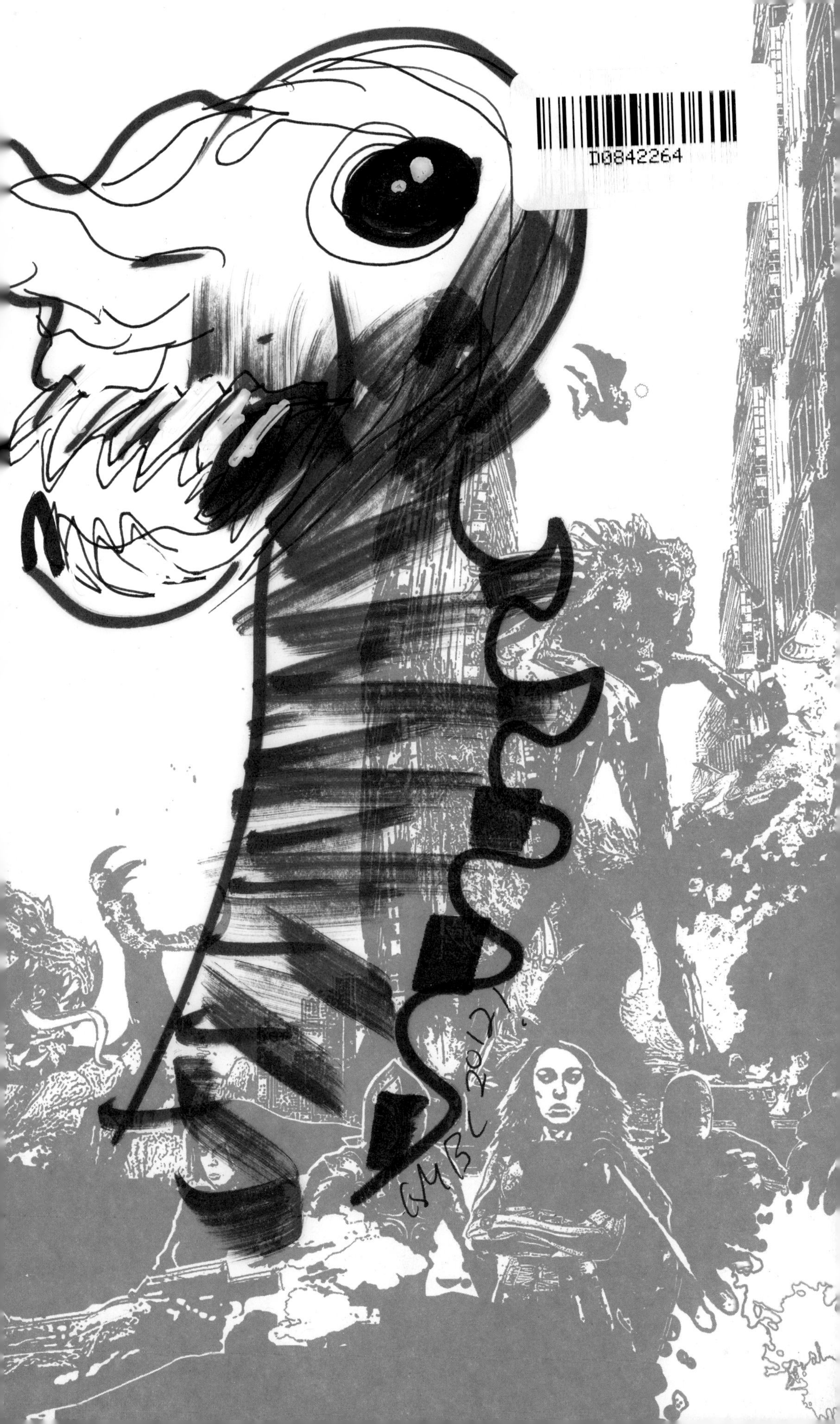
GMB 2012

www.alchemicalpress.com

ALCHEMICAL
PRESS

the IMAGINATION MANIFESTO

book one

Creator- Writer - Illustrator
G.M.B. CHOMICHUK

Cover
GMB Chomichuk and Mike Sanders

Limited Cover
GMB Chomichuk

Contains:

Dedicated to anyone who's had an idea
and then made it real.

Endswell would be impossible without
TMJCM

THE IMAGINATION MANIFESTO: Book One First Printing 2009 ISBN # 978-0-9813550-0-9
Published by Alchemical Press. The Imagination Manifesto, The Tomorrow Society and their related characters are
trademark and copyright GMB Chomichuk and Alchemical Press. Aegri Somnia: A Sick Man's Dreams is Trademark
and copyright James Rewucki, GMB Chomichuk, Absurd Machine Films, Alchemical Press. Sixgun Quixote and its related characters are trademark copyright GMB Chomichuk and John Toone. All characters featured in this work,
names likenesses, and all related indicia are copywright trademark of Alchemical Press and GMB Chomichuk No
similarity between any person place or situation is intended, any such similarity that may exist is purely coincidental.
PRINTED IN CANADA.

the IMAGINATION MANIFESTO

book one

ABOUT THE AUTHORS

G.M.B. Chomichuk is a writer/illustrator living in Winnipeg, Manitoba. He recently worked as Artistic Director on the feature film *AEGRI SOMNIA: A Sick Man's Dreams*, and the first chapter of the graphic novel adaptation is in your hands. In the meantime look for his work on the new Bluewater Productions' Mini-Series *INSANE JANE: THE AVENGING STAR* and in the latest issue of the Calgary literary journal, DANDELION.

John Toone writes picture books like *Catch that Catfish*, *Hope and the Walleye* for his five-year-old son Jackson and three-year-old daughter Gloria. His first collection of poetry, *From Out of Nowhere*, was published by Turnstone Press in spring 2009. He is the past-President of the Manitoba Writers' Guild.

James Rewucki is the president of Absurd Machine Studios and the writer/director of the indie epic film, *AEGRI SOMNIA: A Sick Man's Dreams* and the upcoming graphic novel *Mutare*. He has directed music videos, TV shows, and movies, and is in the process of writing something really scary while you're reading this.

wafer of technology that doesn't exist, or
a slipshod bit of history crammed in to
make things more interesting. And yes
I'm mixing metaphors, because that's
something else all fiction does. It stirs up
all the symbols and images of past and
place, of time and location. The hyper-
real.

THE
IMAGINATION
MANIFESTO

CHAPTER ONE:
BUGHUNT

"...Contemporary man is blind to the fact that, with all his rationality and efficiency, he is possessed by 'powers' that are beyond his control. His gods and demons have not disappeared at all; they have merely got new names... "

-Carl Jung

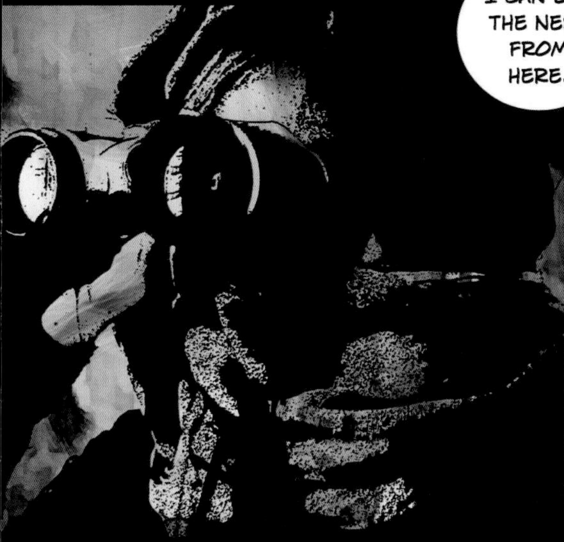

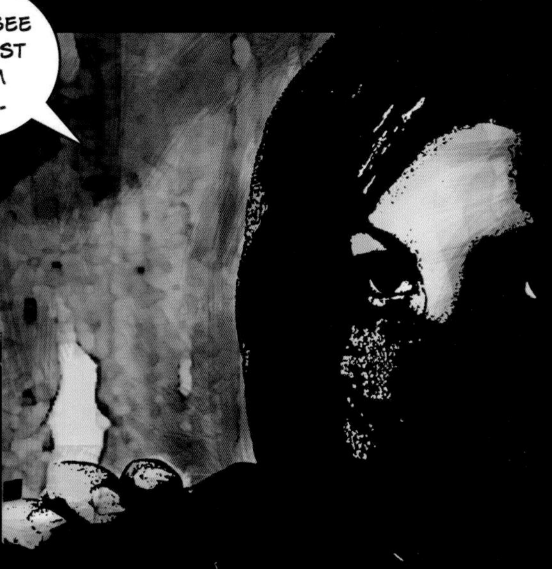
I CAN SEE THE NEST FROM HERE.

rlin. Yesterday.

Endswell has seen this before. In 1954 a hostile national coven used a wyvern in Brussels.

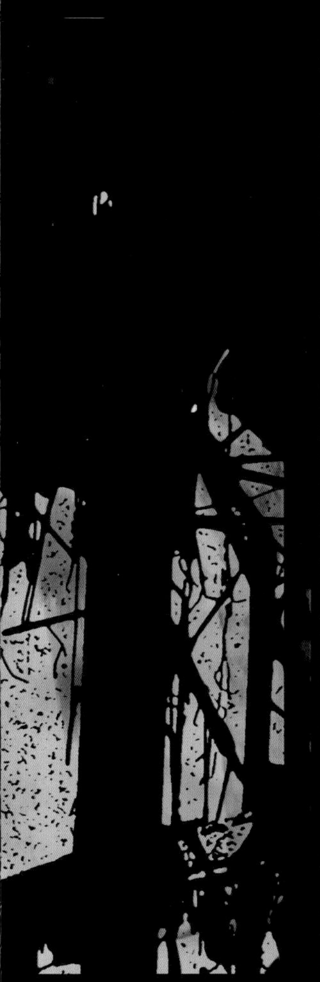

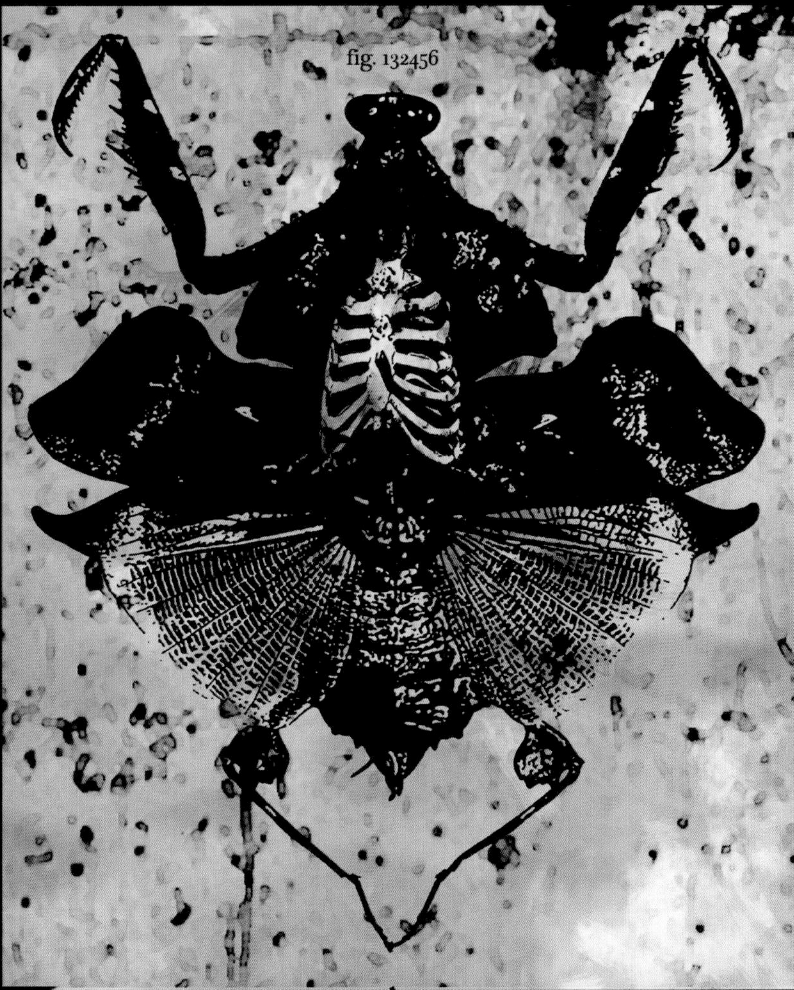
fig. 132456

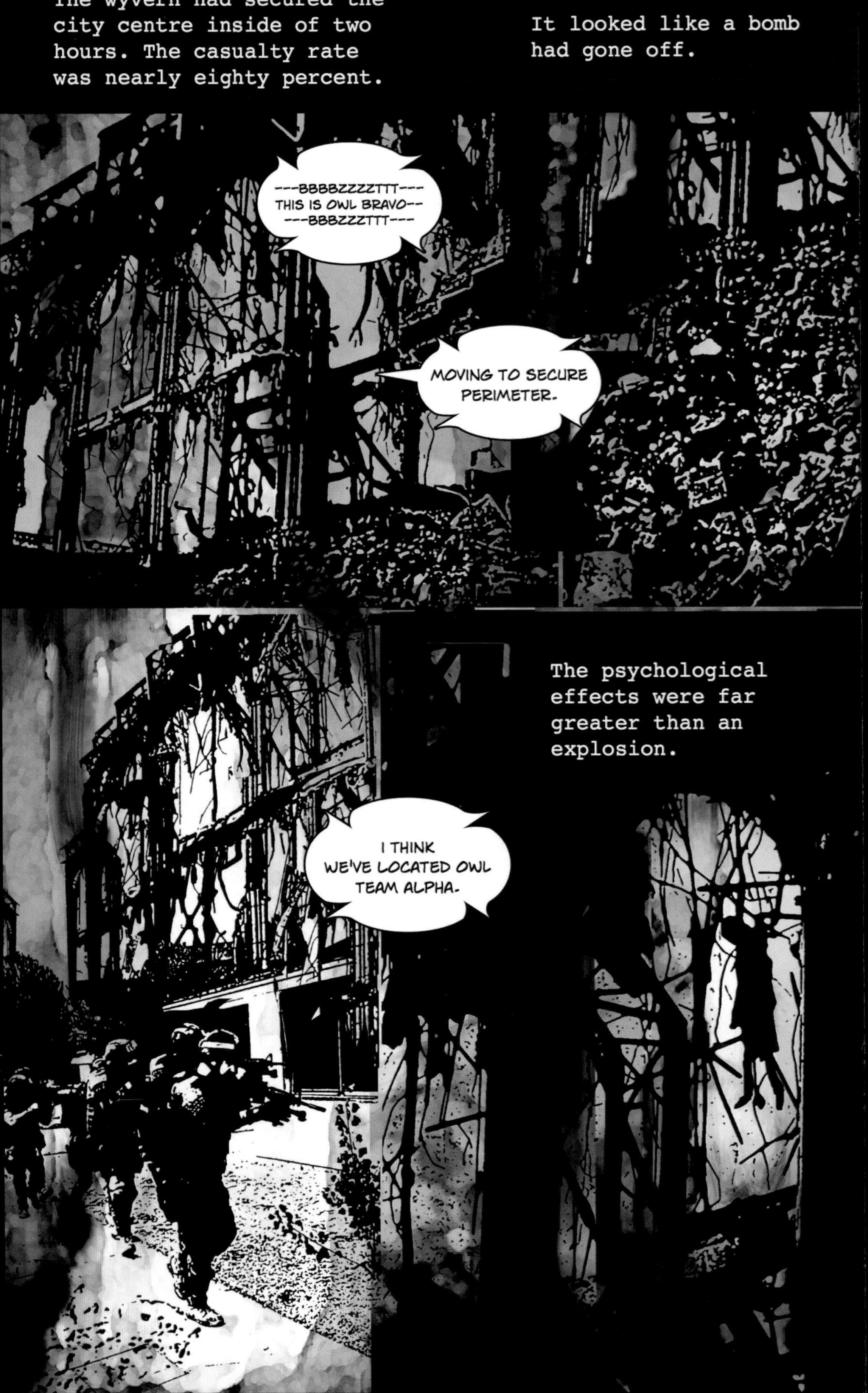
The wyvern had secured the city centre inside of two hours. The casualty rate was nearly eighty percent.
It looked like a bomb had gone off.
---BBBBZZZZTTT--- THIS IS OWL BRAVO-- ---BBBZZZTTT---
MOVING TO SECURE PERIMETER.
The psychological effects were far greater than an explosion.
I THINK WE'VE LOCATED OWL TEAM ALPHA.

Even six weeks after Endswell had killed it...

...the wyvern's victims were still being discovered.

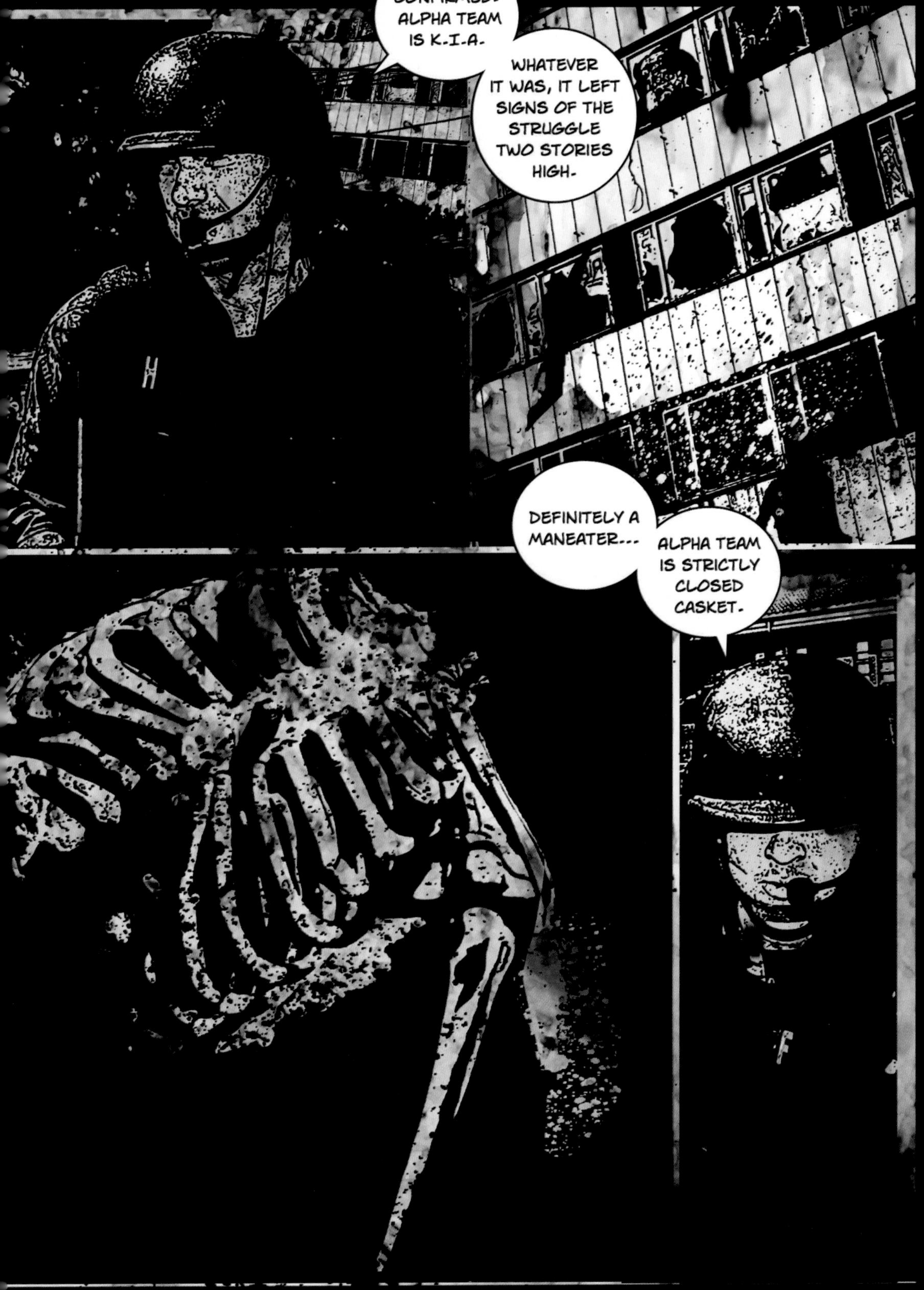

CONFIRMED. ALPHA TEAM IS K.I.A.
WHATEVER IT WAS, IT LEFT SIGNS OF THE STRUGGLE TWO STORIES HIGH.
DEFINITELY A MANEATER...
ALPHA TEAM IS STRICTLY CLOSED CASKET.

Hidden in the rubble, half eaten, rotting, violated.

A bomb doesn't hide a loved one's body on purpose. It doesn't attempt to prolong the events of its own tragic effects.

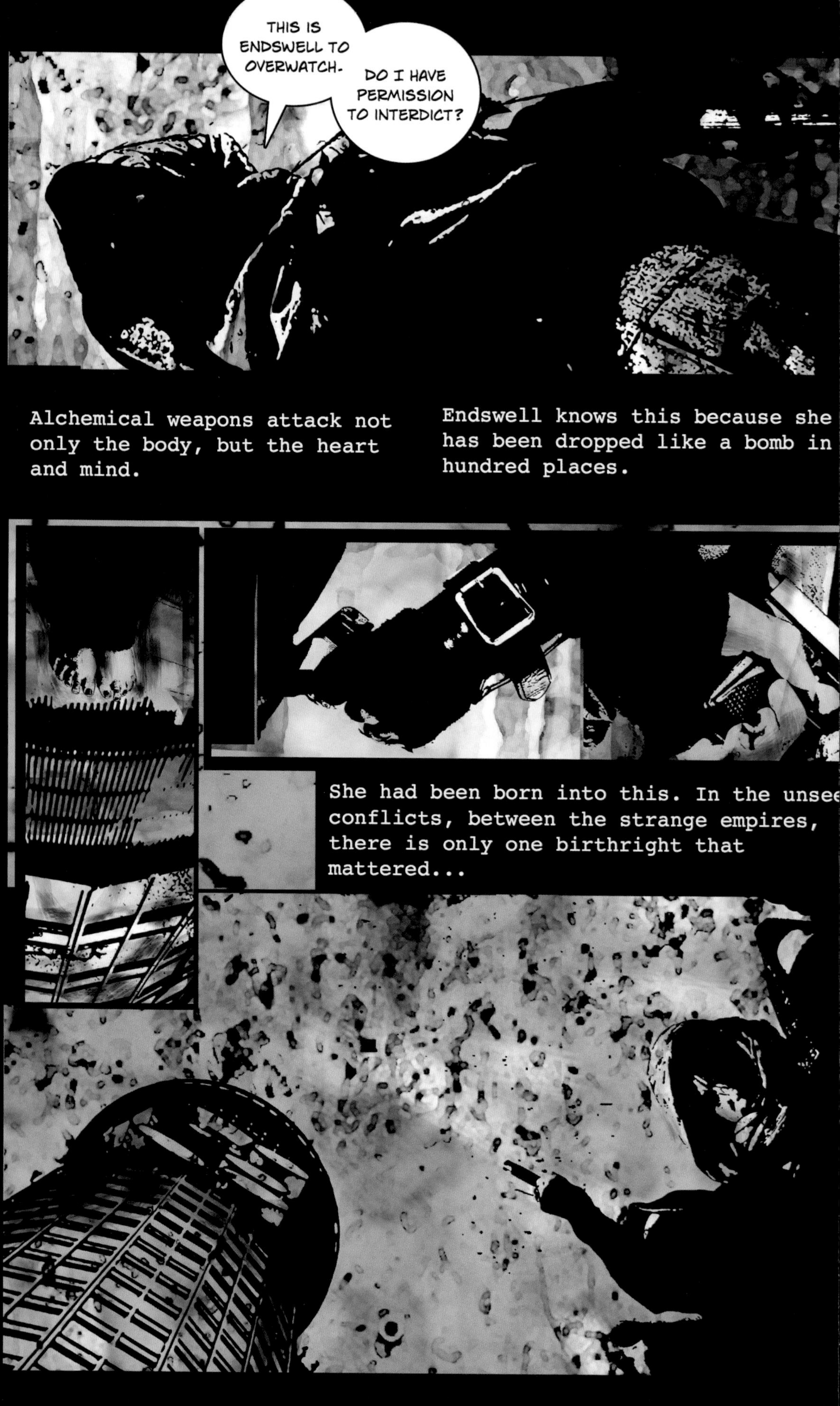
THIS IS ENDSWELL TO OVERWATCH.
DO I HAVE PERMISSION TO INTERDICT?
Alchemical weapons attack not only the body, but the heart and mind.
Endswell knows this because she has been dropped like a bomb in hundred places.
She had been born into this. In the unsee
conflicts, between the strange empires, there is only one birthright that mattered...

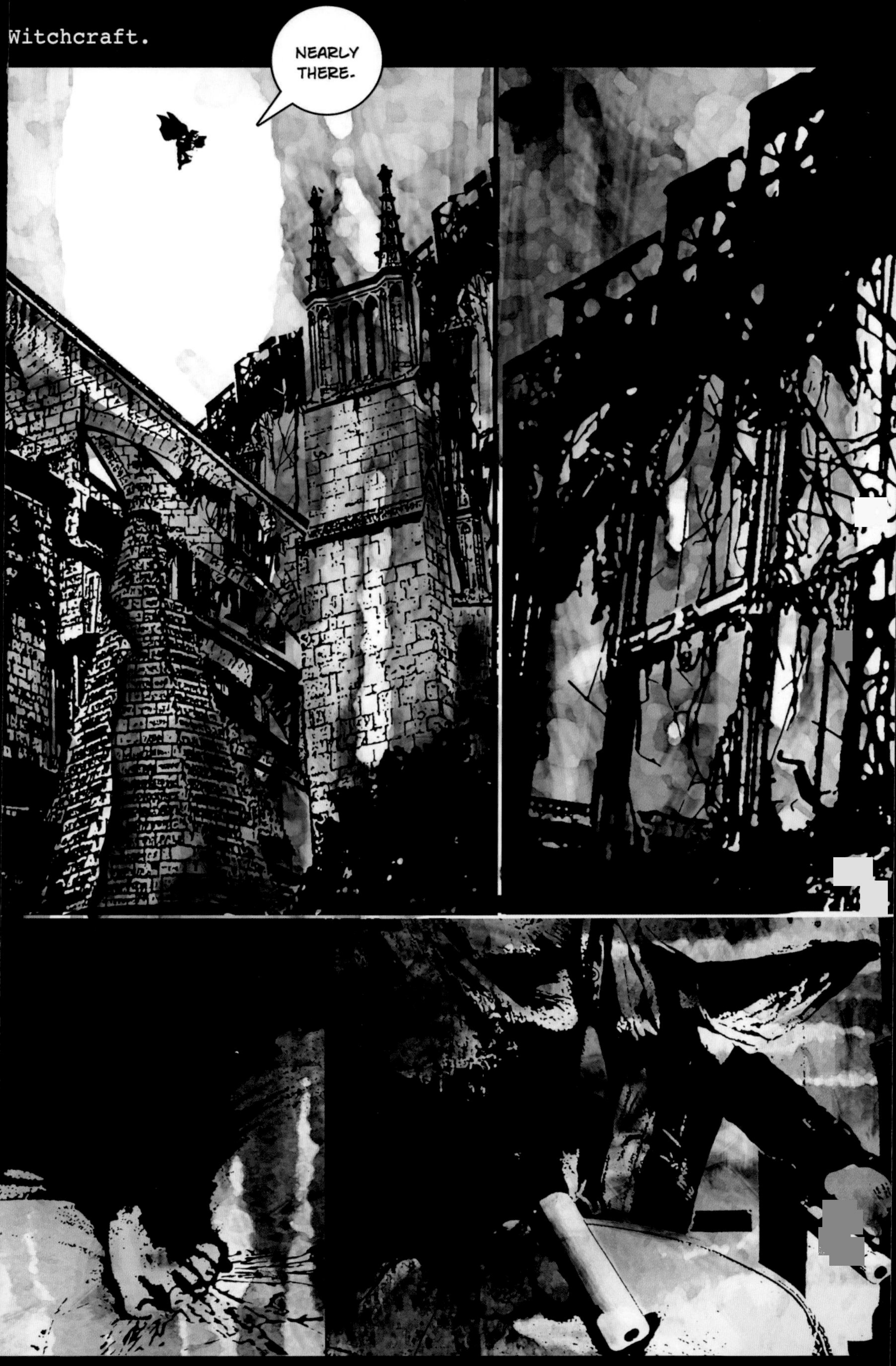
Witchcraft.
NEARLY THERE.

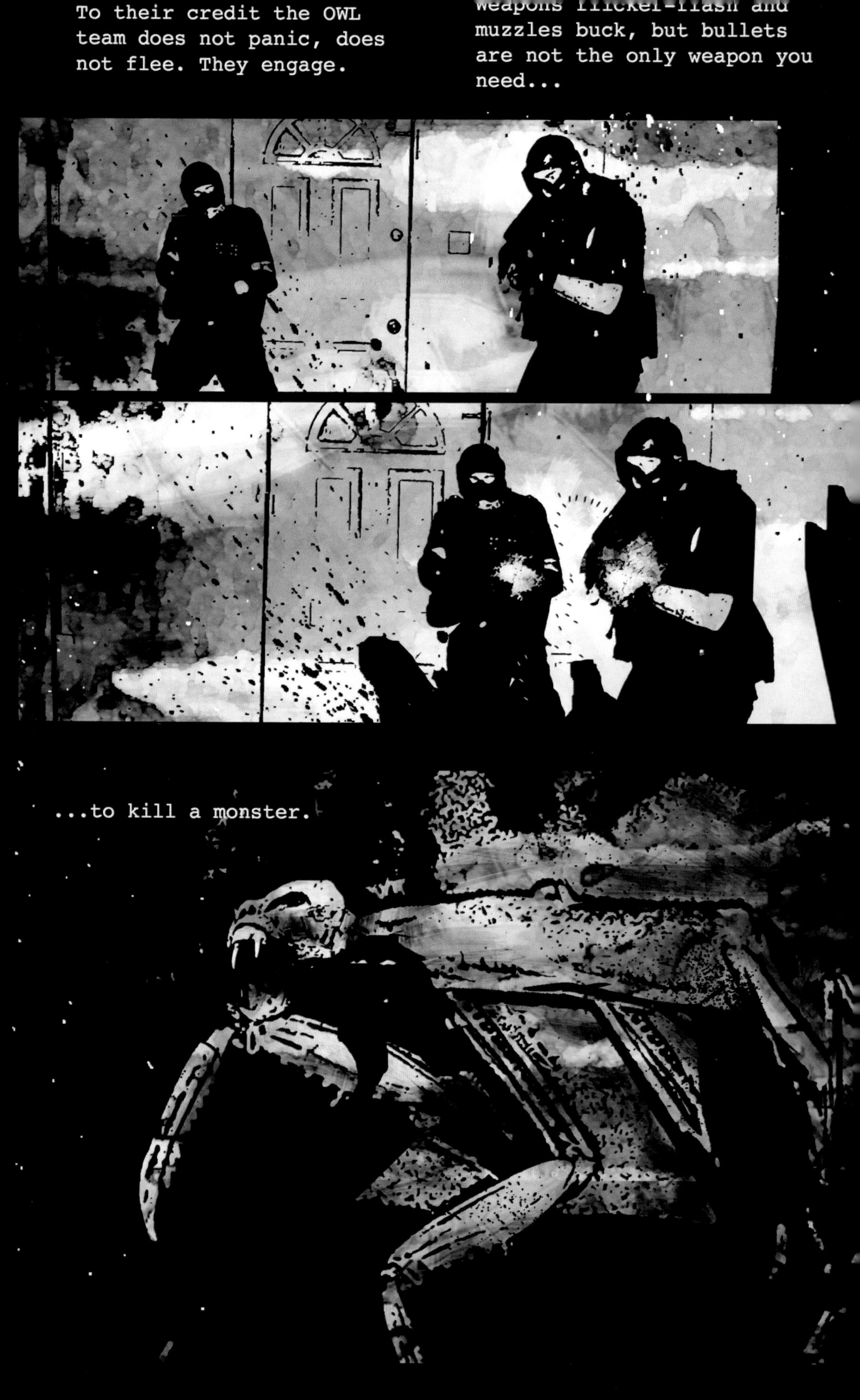
To their credit the OWL team does not panic, does not flee. They engage.
weapons flicker-flash and muzzles buck, but bullets are not the only weapon you need...
...to kill a monster.

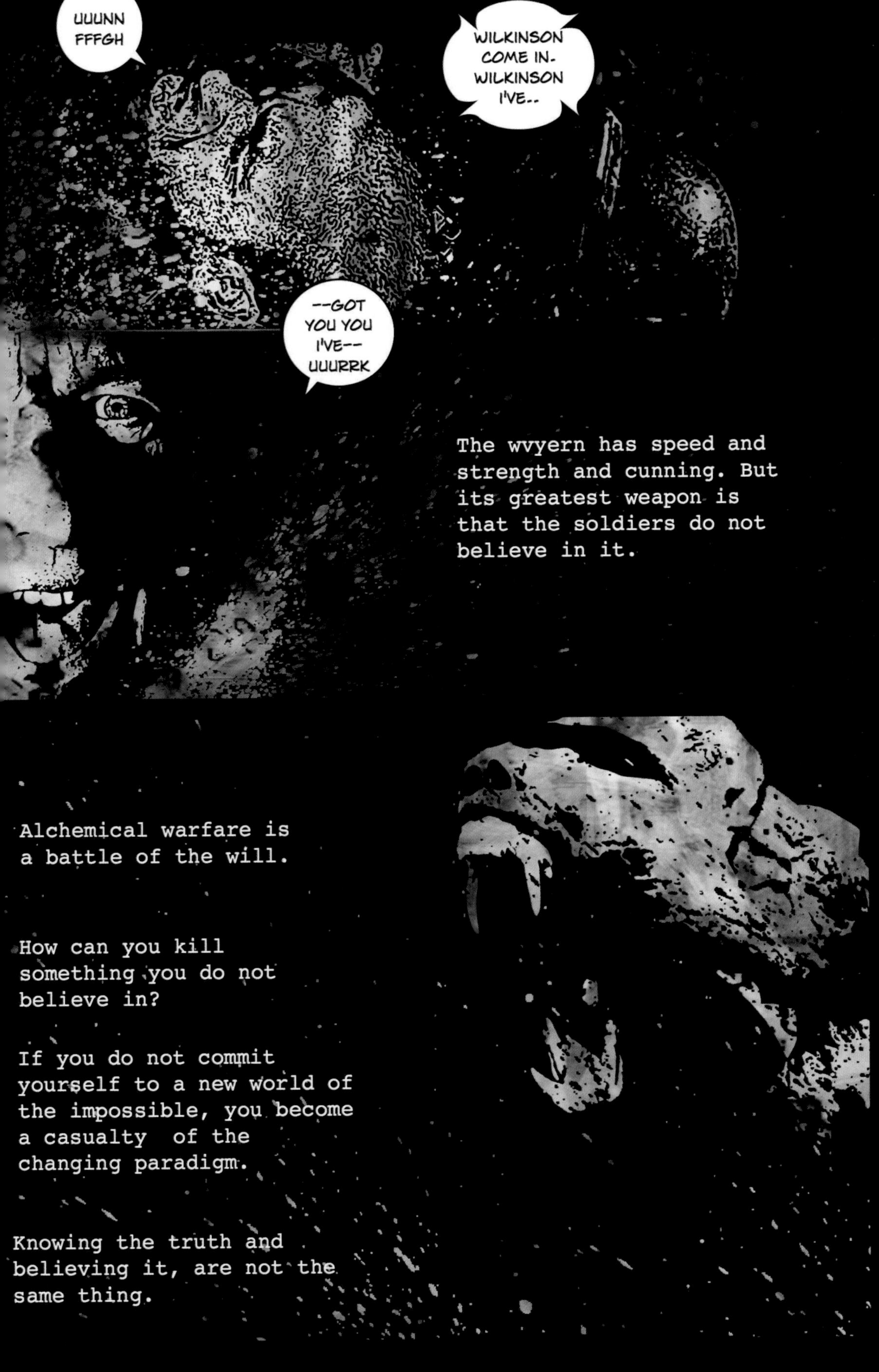
UUUNN FFFGH
WILKINSON COME IN- WILKINSON I'VE..
--GOT YOU YOU I'VE-- UUURRK
The wvyern has speed and strength and cunning. But its greatest weapon is that the soldiers do not believe in it.
Alchemical warfare is a battle of the will.
How can you kill something you do not believe in?
If you do not commit yourself to a new world of the impossible, you become a casualty of the changing paradigm.
Knowing the truth and believing it, are not the same thing.

Truth without belief is as empty as a lie.

Endswell *knows* that she can kill the creature.

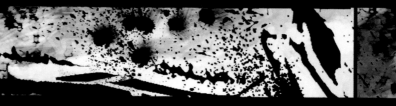

Bullets kick free of their jackets. Buzz like hornets.

Endswell's belief in those tiny agents is a poison. The alchemy of will into action.

The conclusion is not so simple as that...

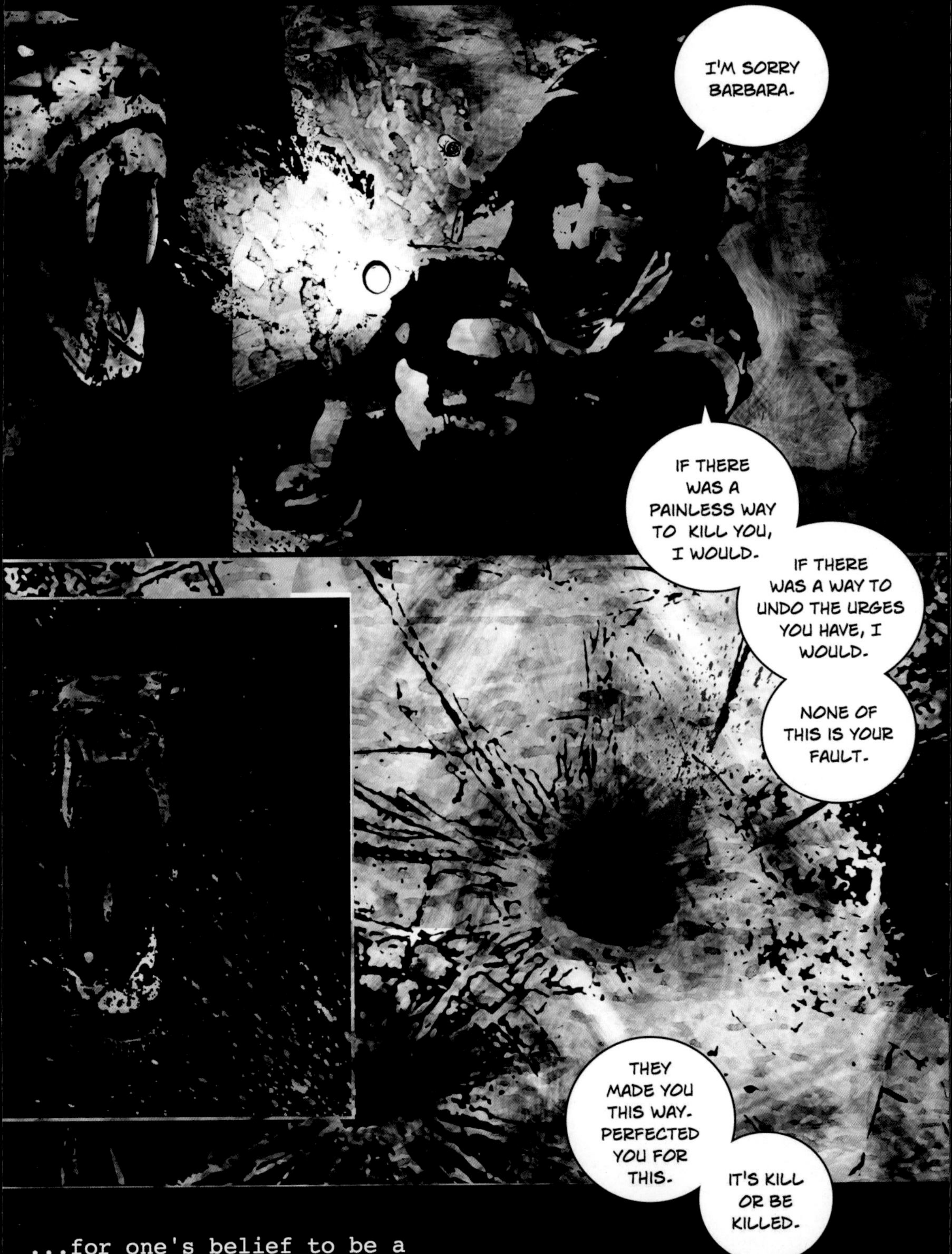
I'M SORRY BARBARA.
IF THERE WAS A PAINLESS WAY TO KILL YOU, I WOULD.
IF THERE WAS A WAY TO UNDO THE URGES YOU HAVE, I WOULD.
NONE OF THIS IS YOUR FAULT.
THEY MADE YOU THIS WAY. PERFECTED YOU FOR THIS.
IT'S KILL OR BE KILLED.

...for one's belief to be a weapon...

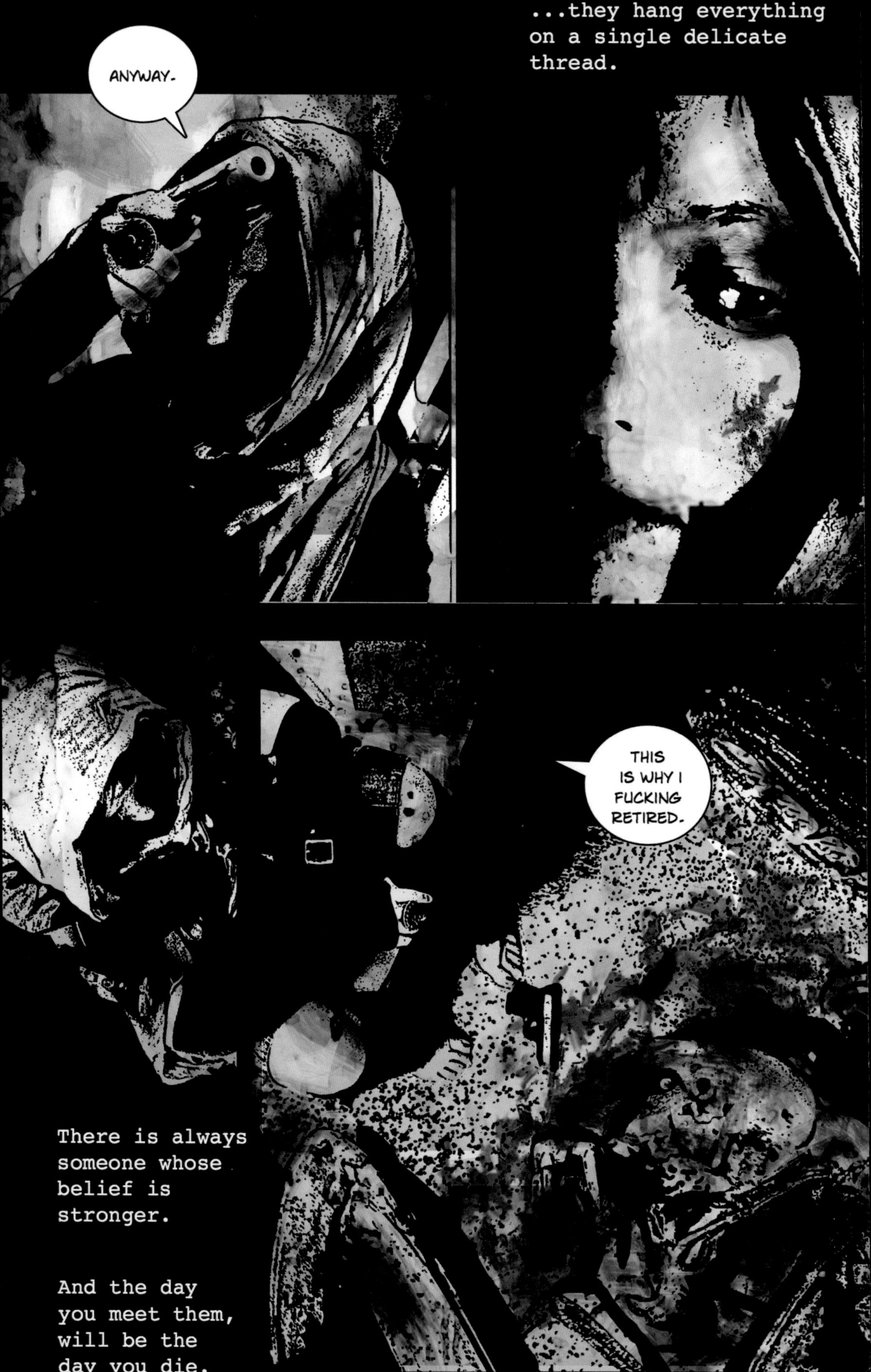
...they hang everything on a single delicate thread.
ANYWAY-
THIS IS WHY I FUCKING RETIRED.
There is always someone whose belief is stronger.
And the day you meet them, will be the day you die.

THE
IMAGINATION
MANIFESTO

CHAPTER TWO:
BULLET

Transatlantic flight.
Praetorian Zepplin. Today.

The sleeping ocean rolls
silently past.

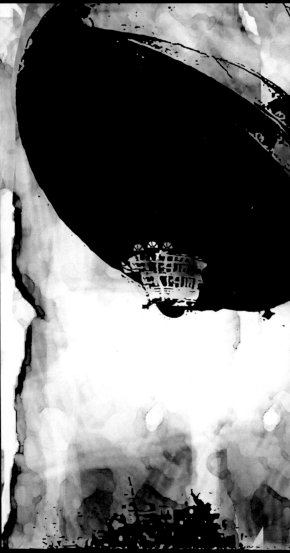

Mr. Candle pulls a long drag
from a dying cigarette.

The hum of motors surge, a
mechanical tide, reminding the
of the great dark water below.

THEY HAVE THEIR LITTLE PIECE OF THE WORLD BACK NOW. THAT'S THE LAST OF THEM THERE.

IT'S STRANGE HOW MANY CAME BACK TO EUROPE AFTER THE WAR AND JUST SETTLED INTO THE RUBBLE.

BUT PEOPLE DON'T FORGET CITIES LIKE BERLIN...TOO CAUGHT UP IN THE SOCIAL CONSCIOUSNESS. I SUPPOSE.

BUT THE REGULAR FOLK CAN GET BACK TO THEIR LIVES...WHAT CAN I DO WITH YOU NOW?

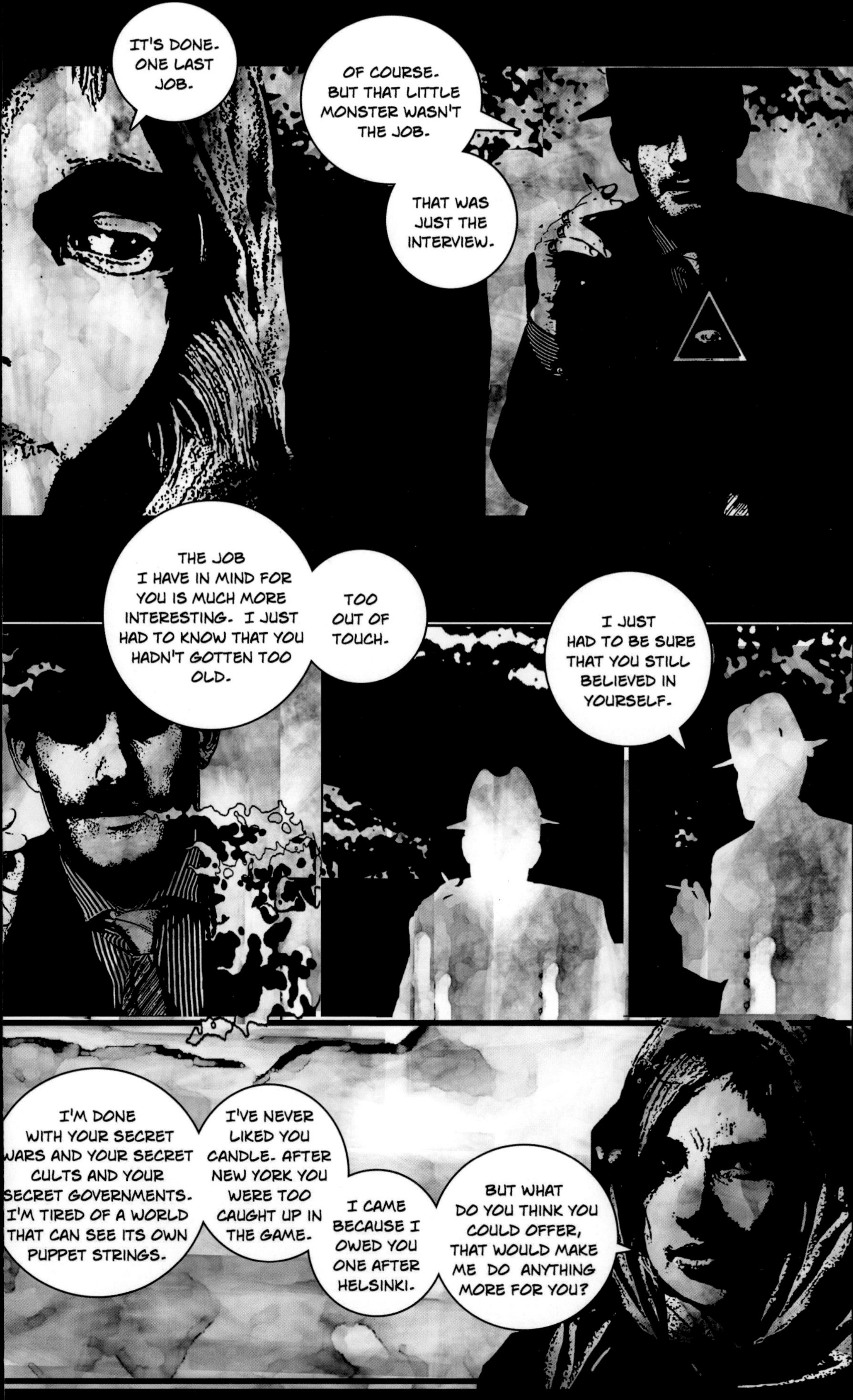
IT'S DONE. ONE LAST JOB.
OF COURSE. BUT THAT LITTLE MONSTER WASN'T THE JOB.
THAT WAS JUST THE INTERVIEW.
THE JOB I HAVE IN MIND FOR YOU IS MUCH MORE INTERESTING. I JUST HAD TO KNOW THAT YOU HADN'T GOTTEN TOO OLD.
TOO OUT OF TOUCH.
I JUST HAD TO BE SURE THAT YOU STILL BELIEVED IN YOURSELF.
I'M DONE WITH YOUR SECRET WARS AND YOUR SECRET CULTS AND YOUR SECRET GOVERNMENTS. I'M TIRED OF A WORLD THAT CAN SEE ITS OWN PUPPET STRINGS.
I'VE NEVER LIKED YOU CANDLE. AFTER NEW YORK YOU WERE TOO CAUGHT UP IN THE GAME.
I CAME BECAUSE I OWED YOU ONE AFTER HELSINKI.
BUT WHAT DO YOU THINK YOU COULD OFFER, THAT WOULD MAKE ME DO ANYTHING MORE FOR YOU?

A CLUE.
A WAY TO SOLVE THE ONLY MYSTERY THAT EVER MATTERED TO YOU.

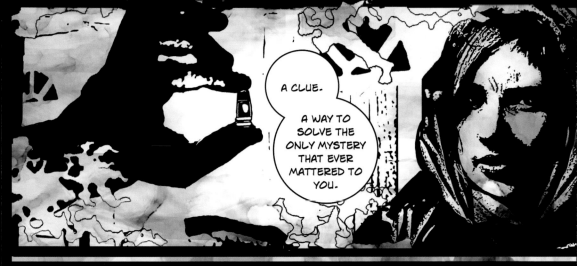

Endswell cannot forget the smell of the crowd. The secret people of the earth awash in cinnamon and incense. The trappings of rites and passages of ancient unknown things.

"You look nervous," Said the Queen.

"Only cautious," Endswell said.

"You worry for nothing. Nothing can harm me, for no one believes tha[redacted]they can. No one can reach me[redacted]try because I believe that nothing made to harm me can escape your notice. Belief is our sword and shield."

"I do not doubt it."

"Good that you do not."

Then she died. Her chest caving inward from the force of the shot, and behind her the great wet wash of her life's blood speckling the faces of her ladies in waiting.

Endswell. Guardian of the Queen o[redacted] World. Witness to the murde[redacted]hat changed the world. She stood there for a long time. Not believing she had failed.

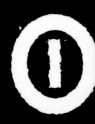

CHAPTER THREE:
SMALL TOWN WIZARDS

Little corners of the world that people can't remember. Places people were made to forget.

the truce. Don't worry you will be left to live in peace."

That's what they always say.

What they don't say: "You'll get the places no one would ever want."

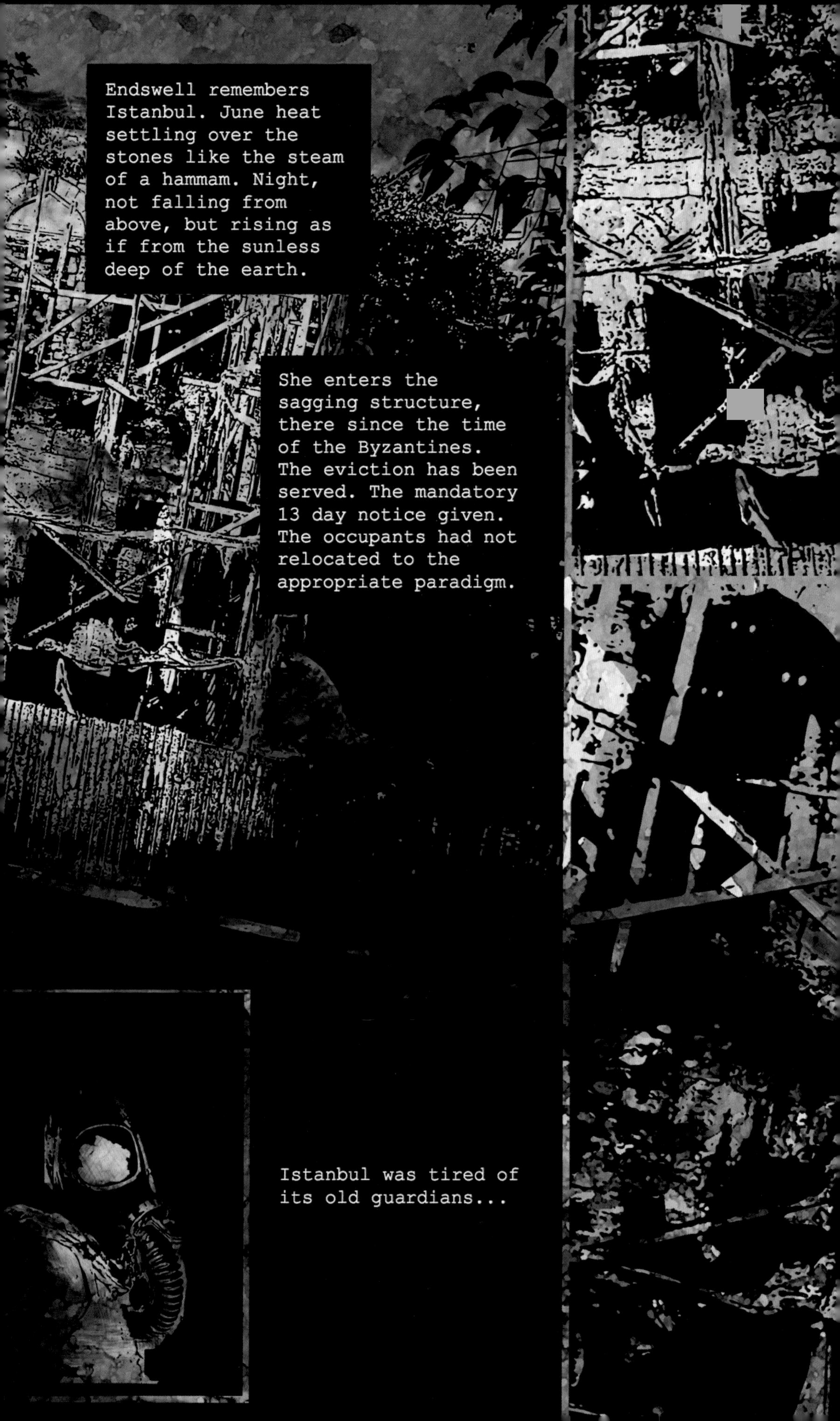
Endswell remembers Istanbul. June heat settling over the stones like the steam of a hammam. Night, not falling from above, but rising as if from the sunless deep of the earth.
She enters the sagging structure, there since the time of the Byzantines. The eviction has been served. The mandatory 13 day notice given. The occupants had not relocated to the appropriate paradigm.
Istanbul was tired of its old guardians...

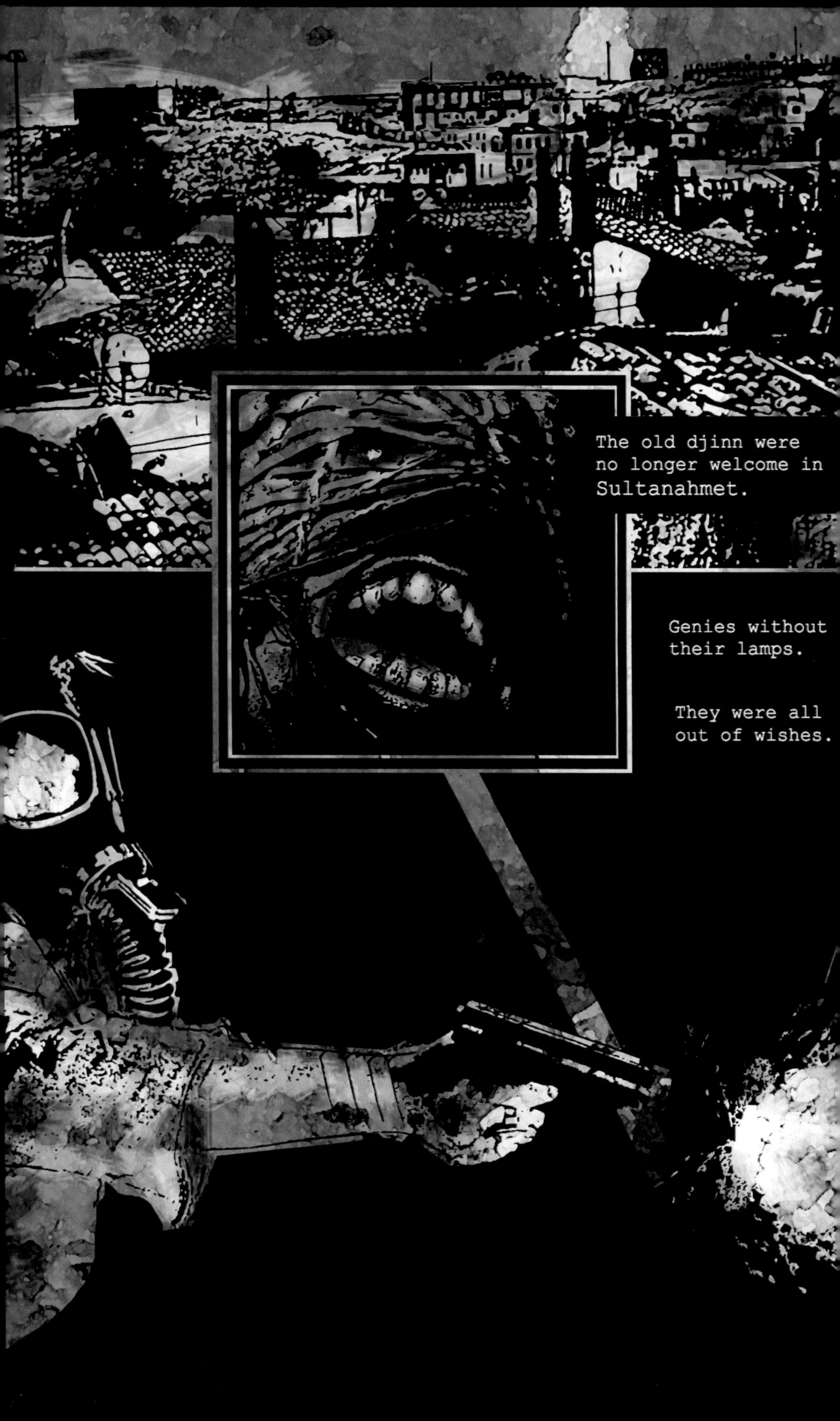
The old djinn were no longer welcome in Sultanahmet.
Genies without their lamps.
They were all out of wishes.

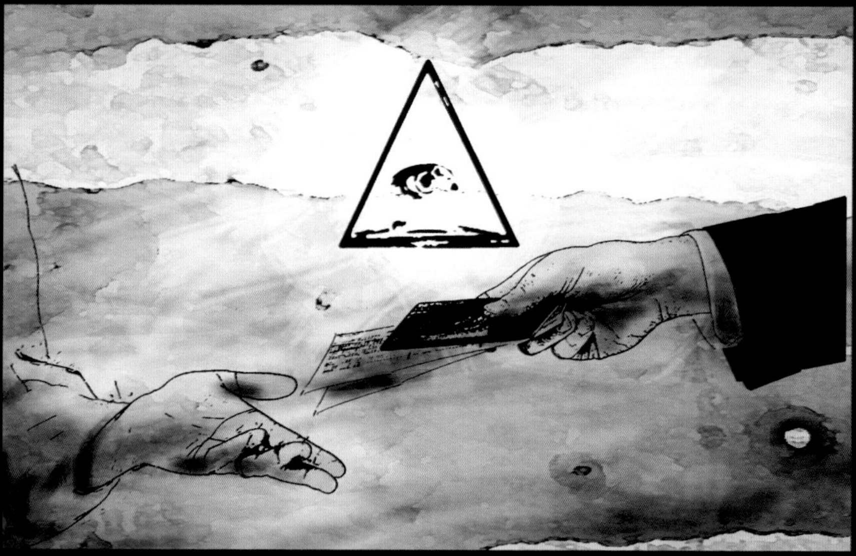

The customs officer has had too much plastic surgery.

"Everything seems to be in order. Just remember that when you cross that bridge you are leaving the prescribed paradigm."

"I know your credentials say that you have access, but I would be remiss to let you cross that bridge without telling you...."

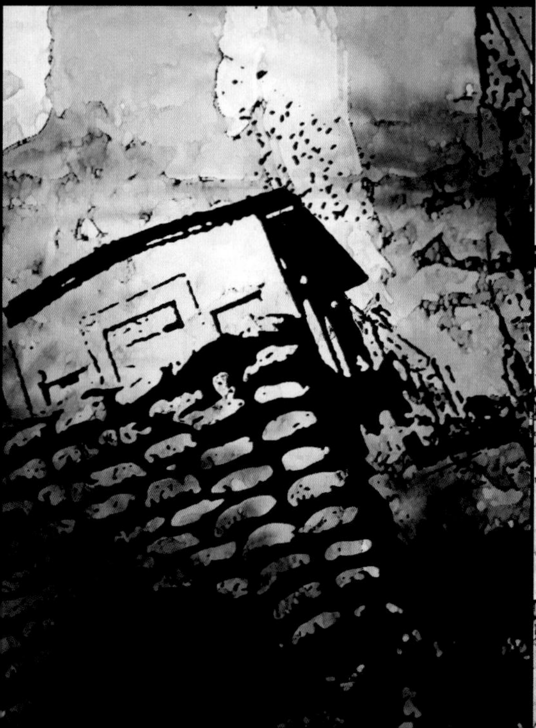

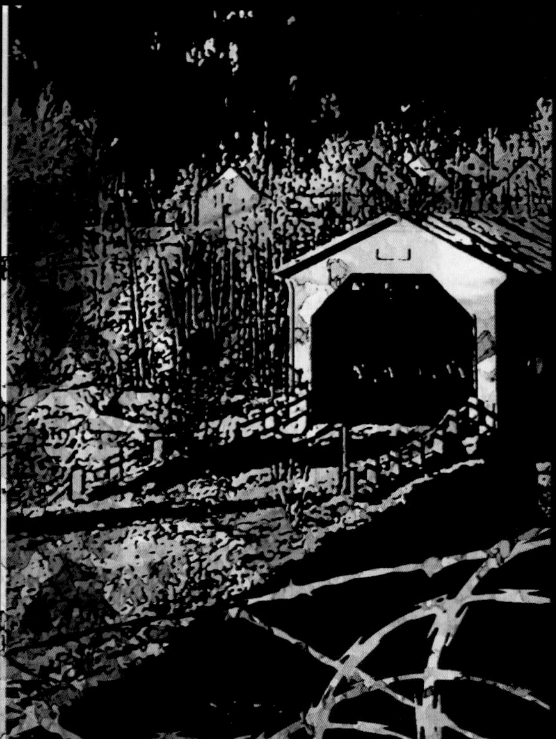

...that things are very different on the reserves."

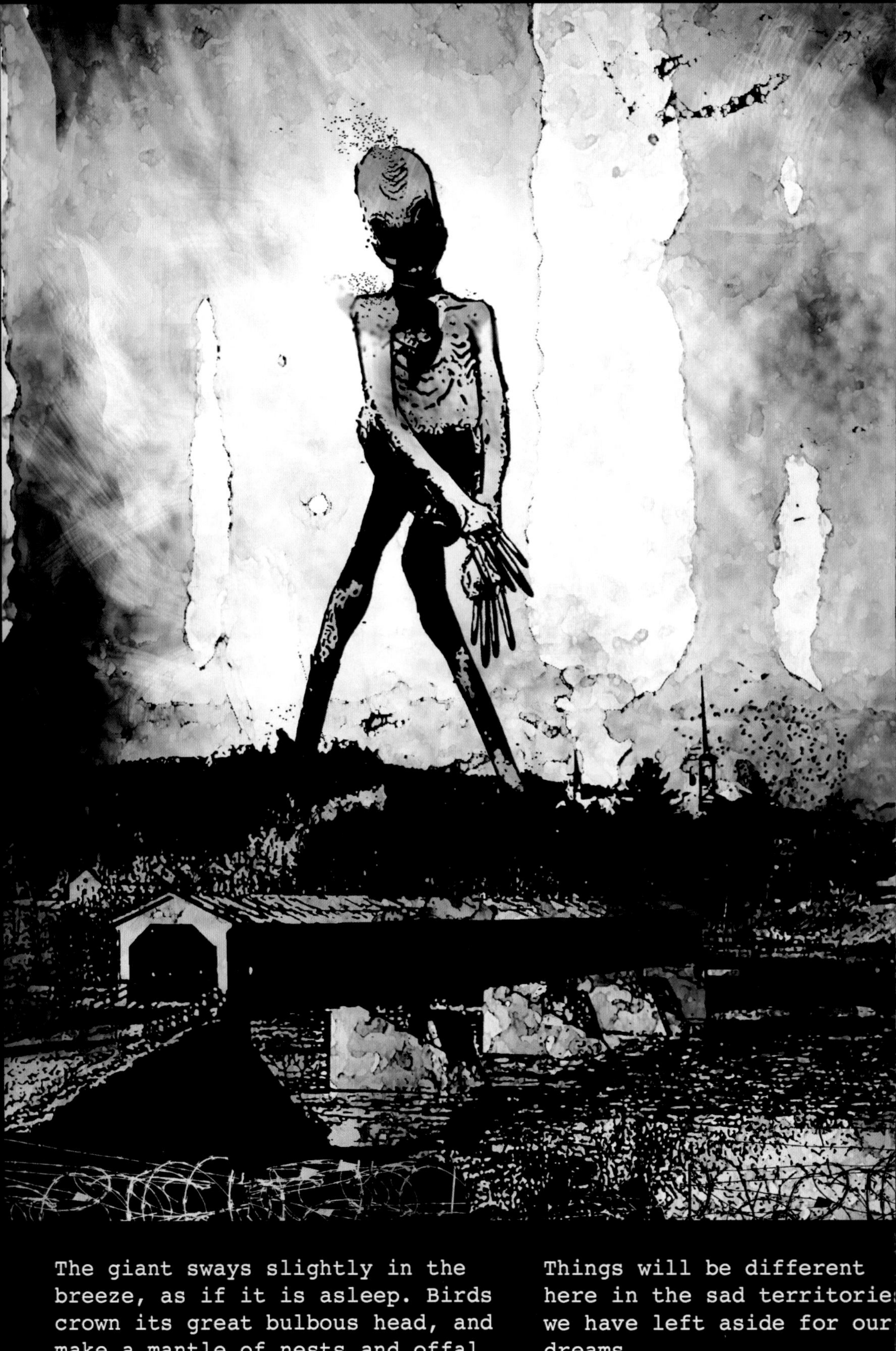

The giant sways slightly in the breeze, as if it is asleep. Birds crown its great bulbous head, and make a mantle of nests and offal

Things will be different here in the sad territories we have left aside for our dreams.

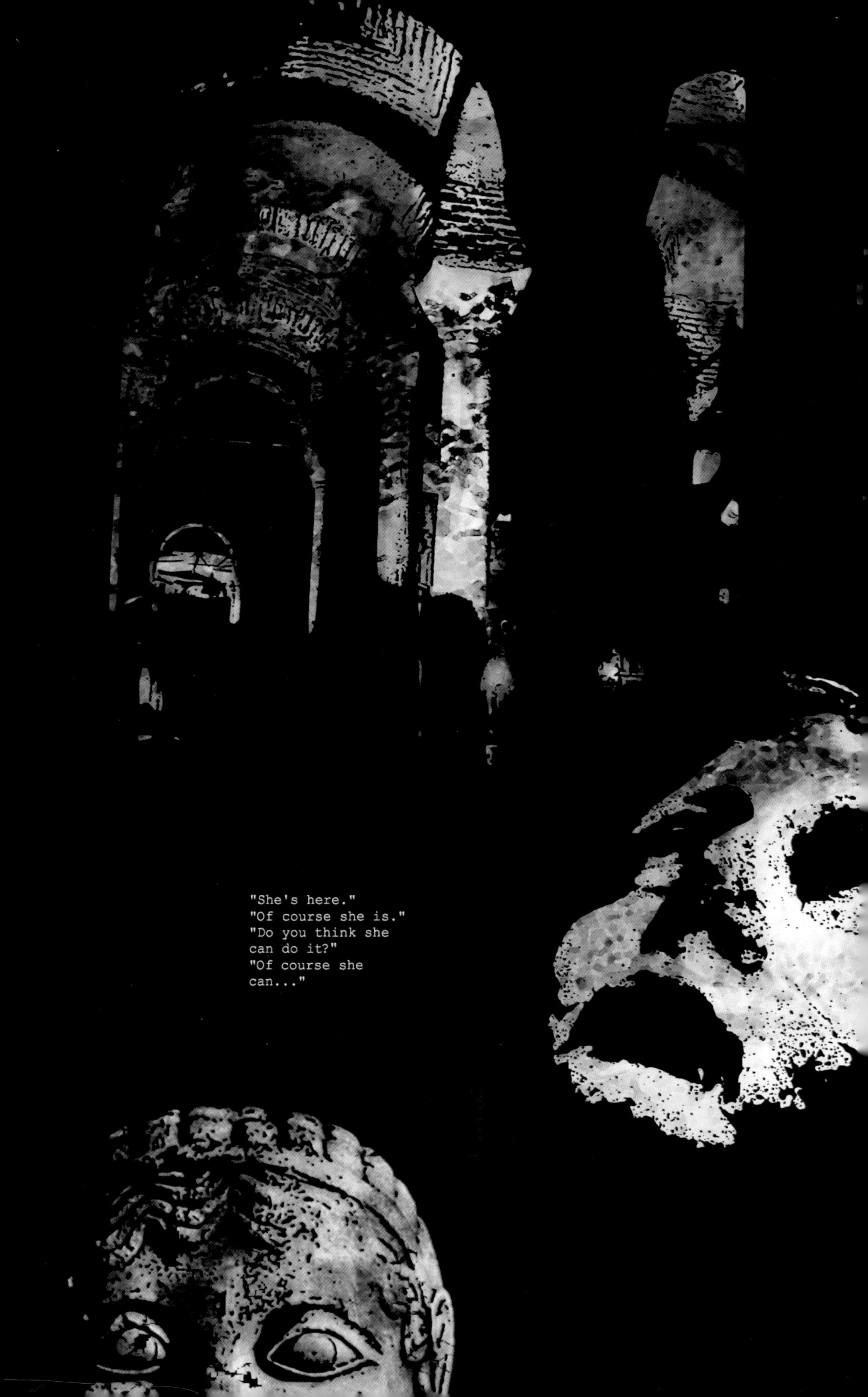

"She's here."
"Of course she is."
"Do you think she
can do it?"
"Of course she
can..."

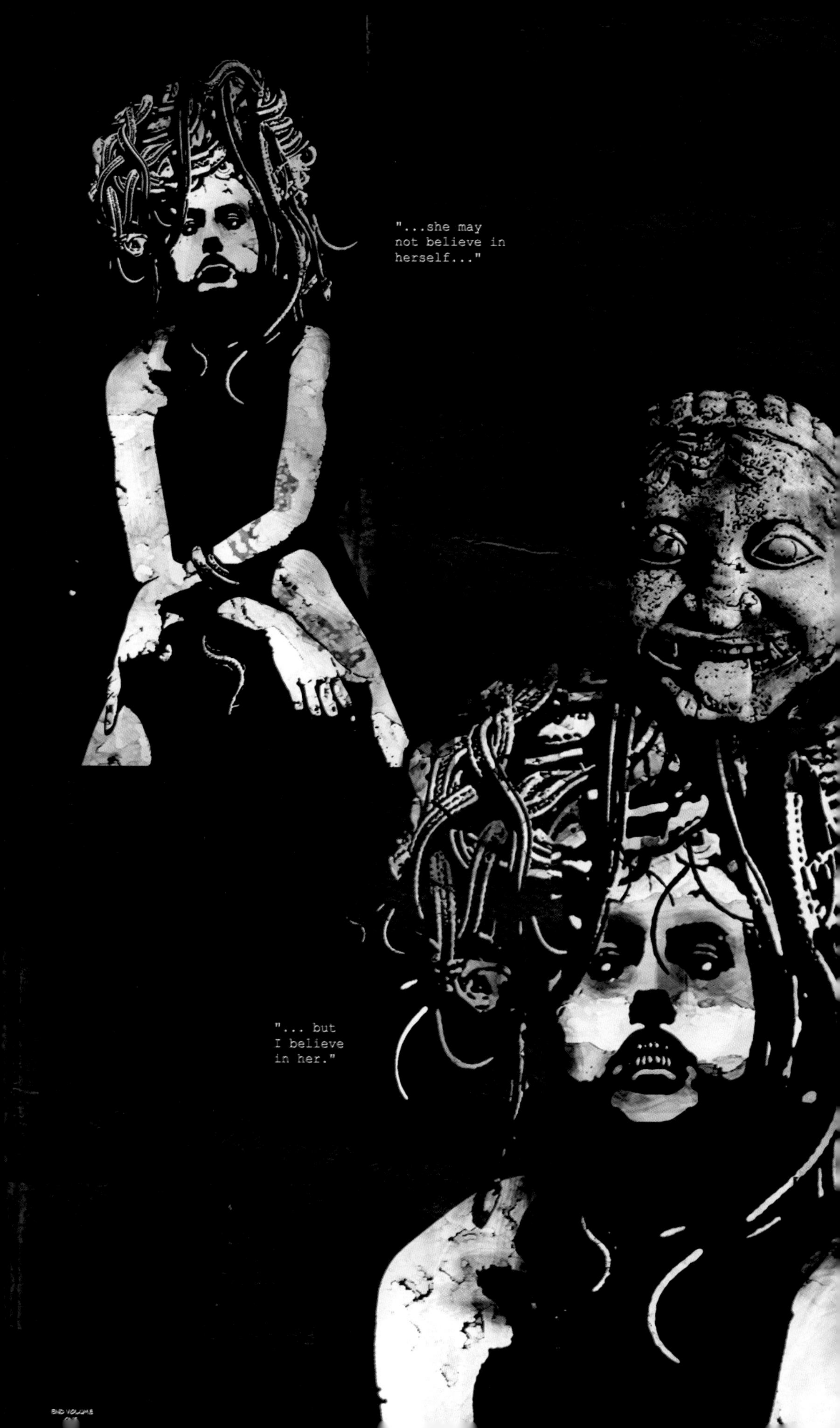
"...she may not believe in herself..."
"... but I believe in her."
END VOLUME

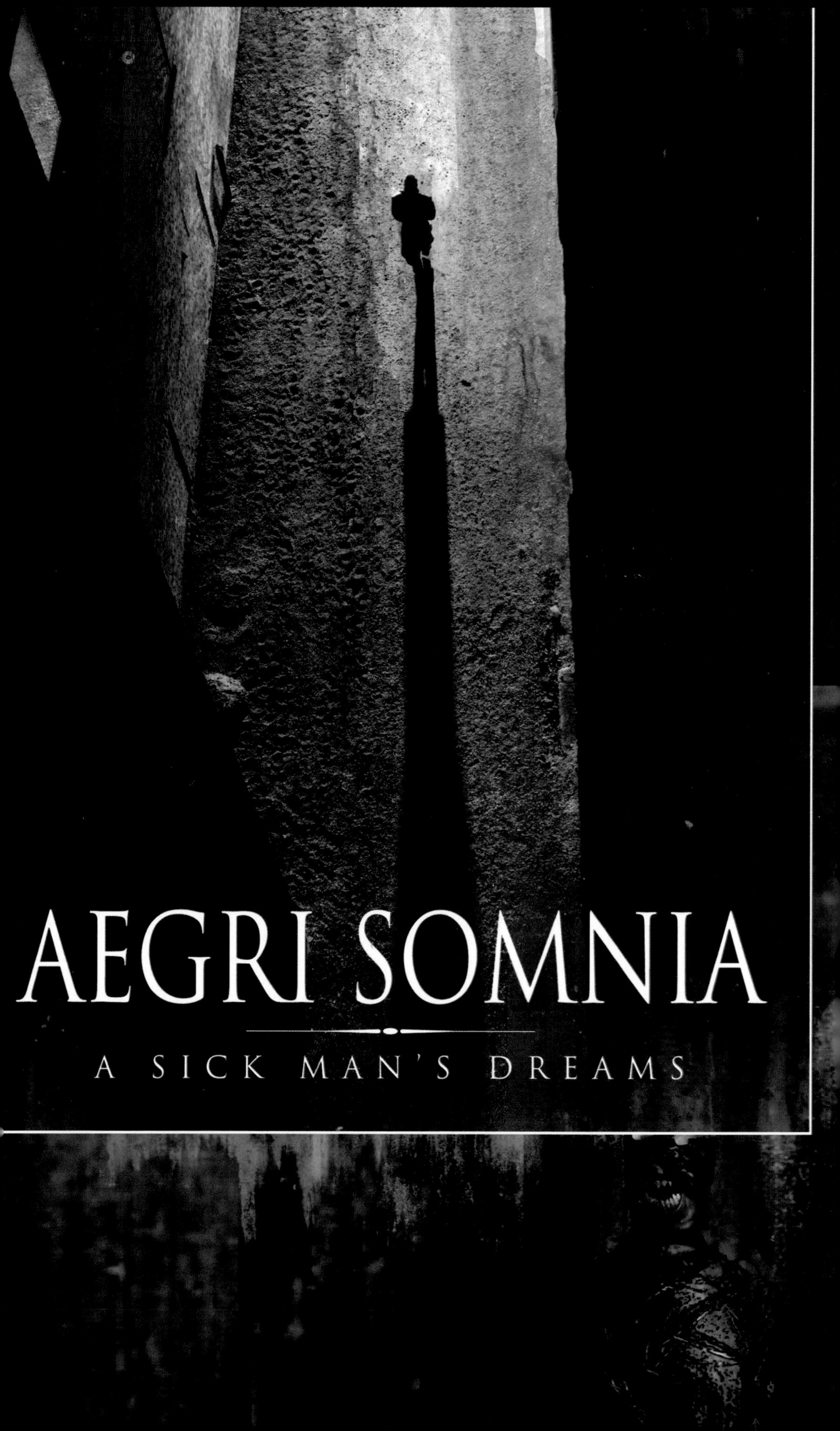
AEGRI SOMNIA
A SICK MAN'S DREAMS

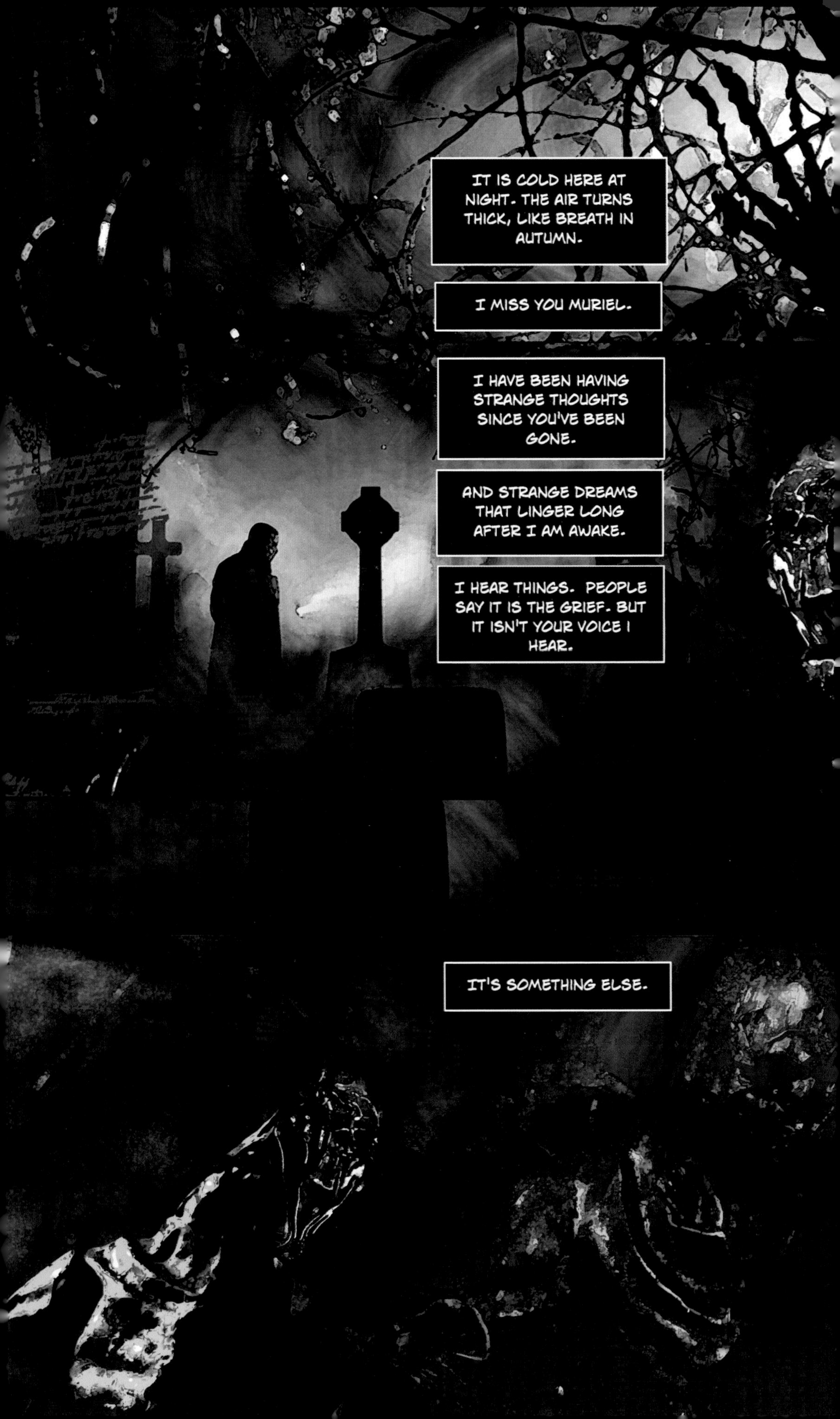
IT IS COLD HERE AT NIGHT. THE AIR TURNS THICK, LIKE BREATH IN AUTUMN.
I MISS YOU MURIEL.
I HAVE BEEN HAVING STRANGE THOUGHTS SINCE YOU'VE BEEN GONE.
AND STRANGE DREAMS THAT LINGER LONG AFTER I AM AWAKE.
I HEAR THINGS. PEOPLE SAY IT IS THE GRIEF. BUT IT ISN'T YOUR VOICE I HEAR.
IT'S SOMETHING ELSE.

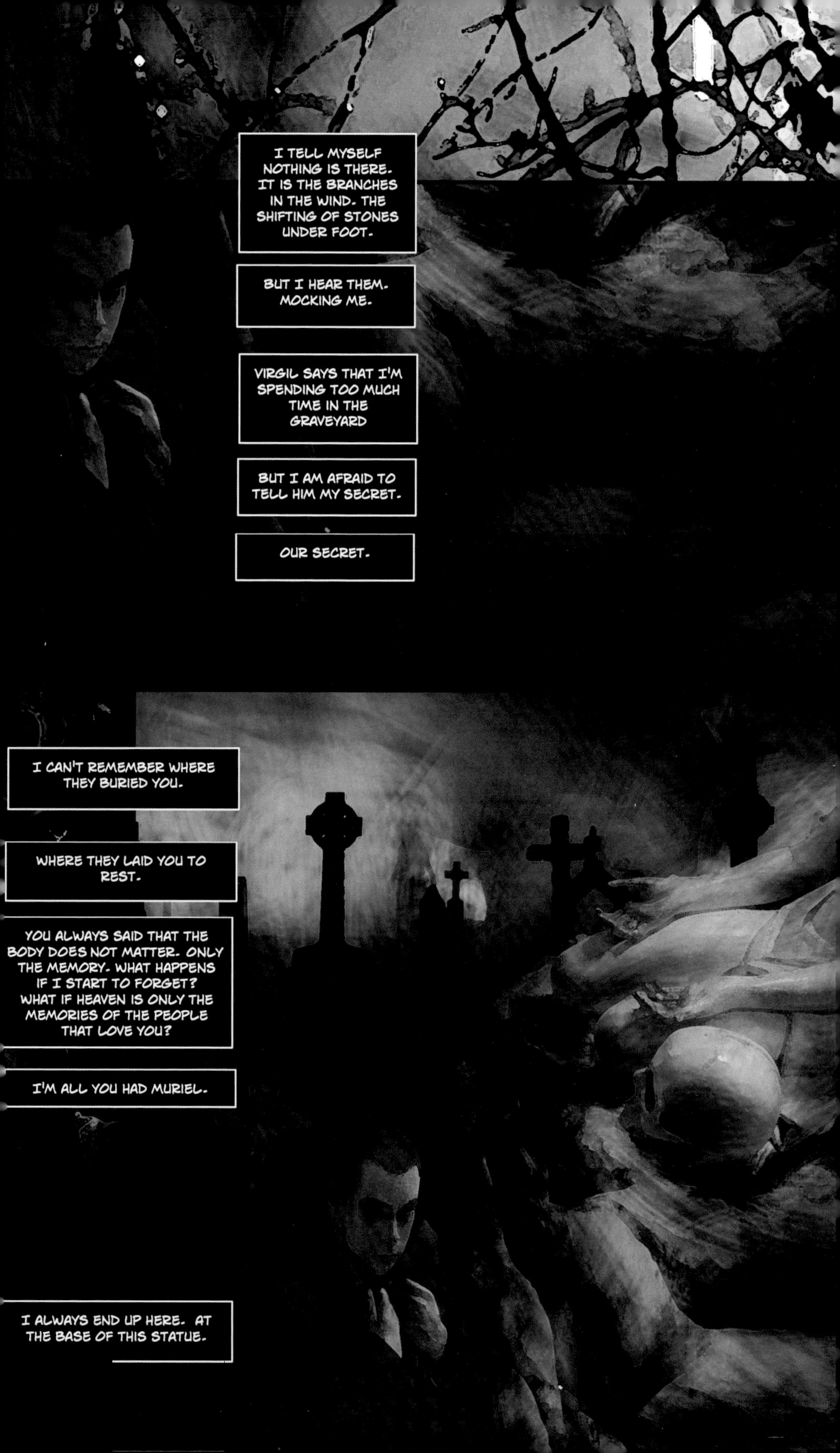
I TELL MYSELF NOTHING IS THERE. IT IS THE BRANCHES IN THE WIND. THE SHIFTING OF STONES UNDER FOOT.
BUT I HEAR THEM. MOCKING ME.
VIRGIL SAYS THAT I'M SPENDING TOO MUCH TIME IN THE GRAVEYARD
BUT I AM AFRAID TO TELL HIM MY SECRET.
OUR SECRET.
I CAN'T REMEMBER WHERE THEY BURIED YOU.
WHERE THEY LAID YOU TO REST.
YOU ALWAYS SAID THAT THE BODY DOES NOT MATTER. ONLY THE MEMORY. WHAT HAPPENS IF I START TO FORGET? WHAT IF HEAVEN IS ONLY THE MEMORIES OF THE PEOPLE THAT LOVE YOU?
I'M ALL YOU HAD MURIEL.
I ALWAYS END UP HERE. AT THE BASE OF THIS STATUE.

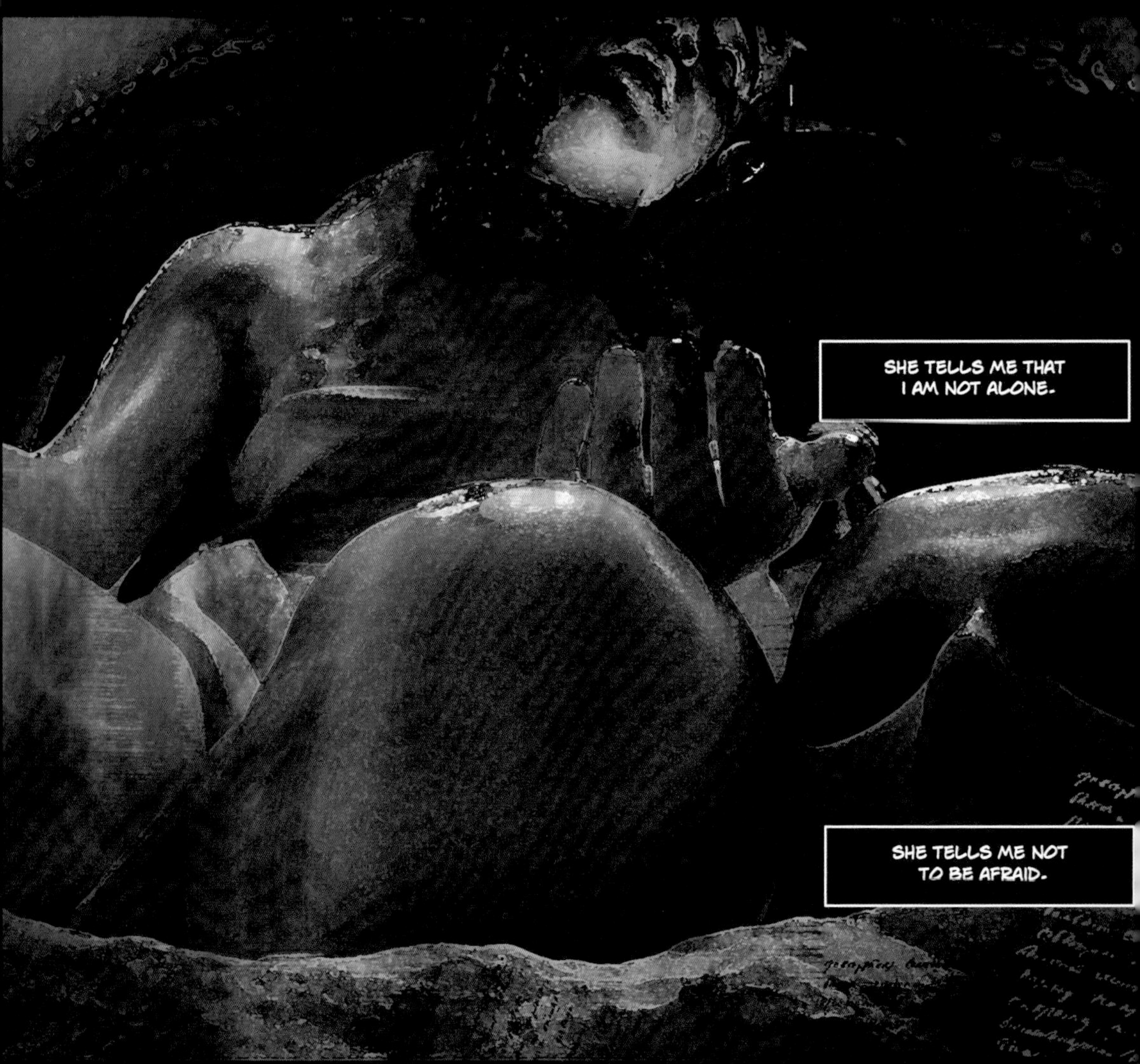
SHE TELLS ME THAT I AM NOT ALONE.
SHE TELLS ME NOT TO BE AFRAID.

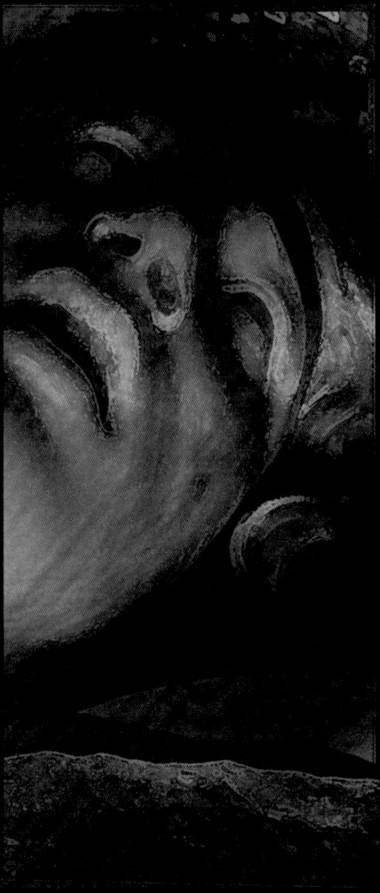

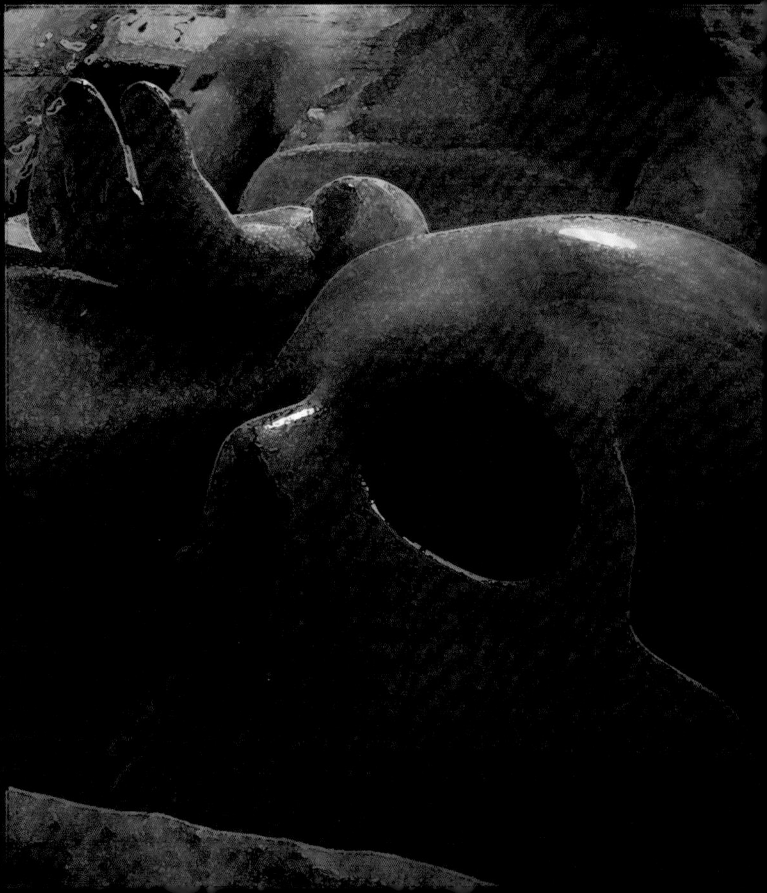

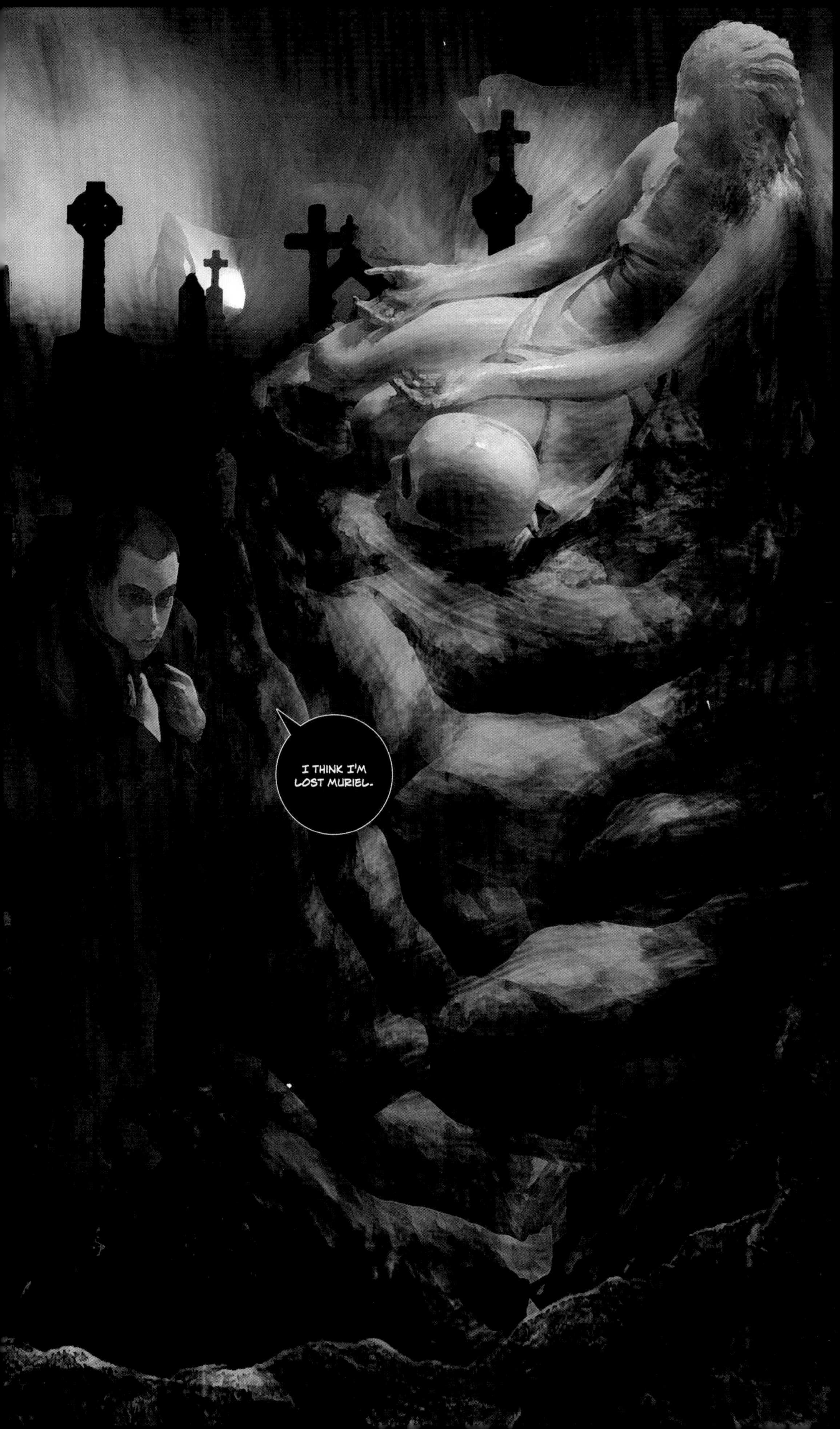
I THINK I'M LOST MURIEL.

...there
...the path of light walk
shadow.

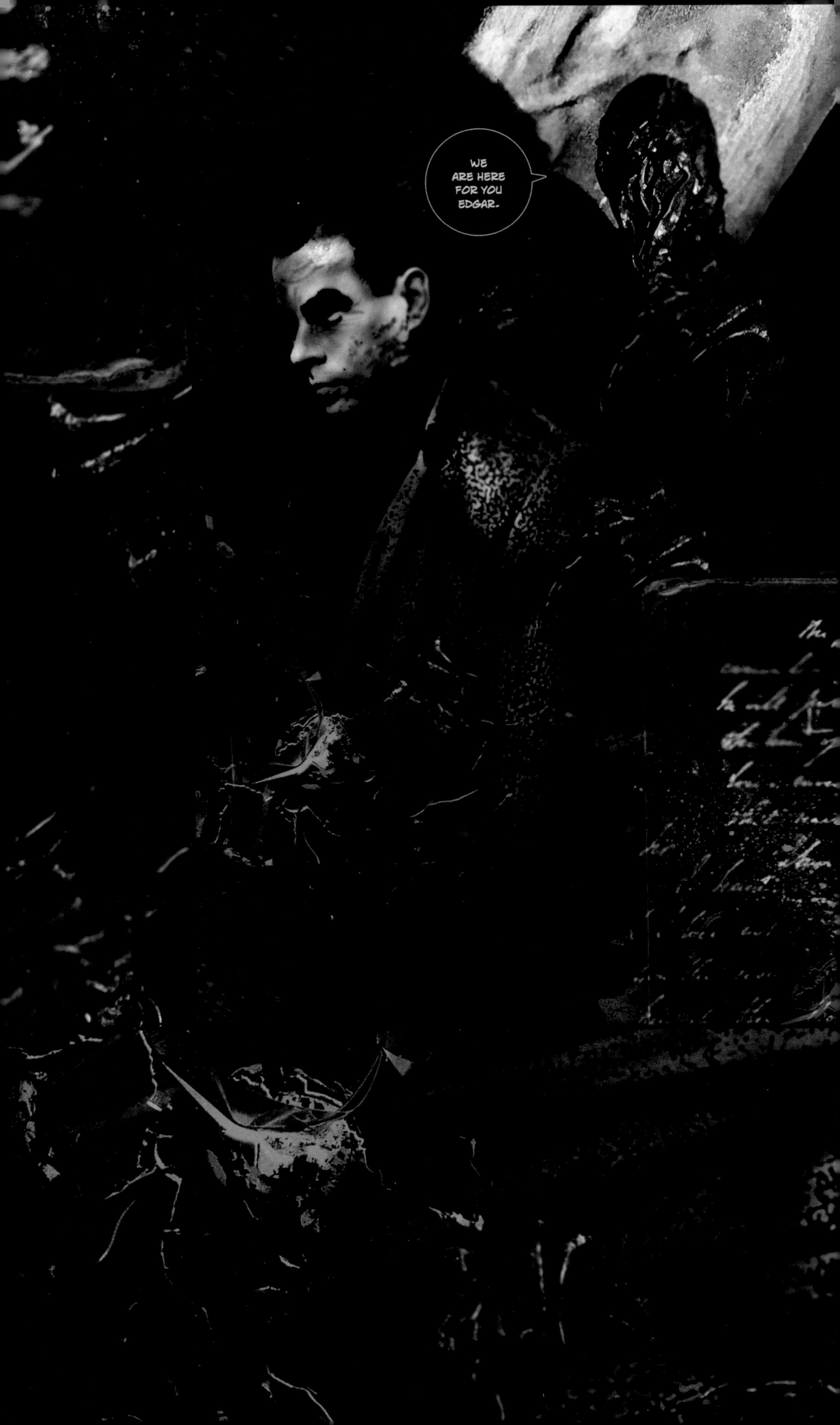
WE ARE HERE FOR YOU EDGAR.

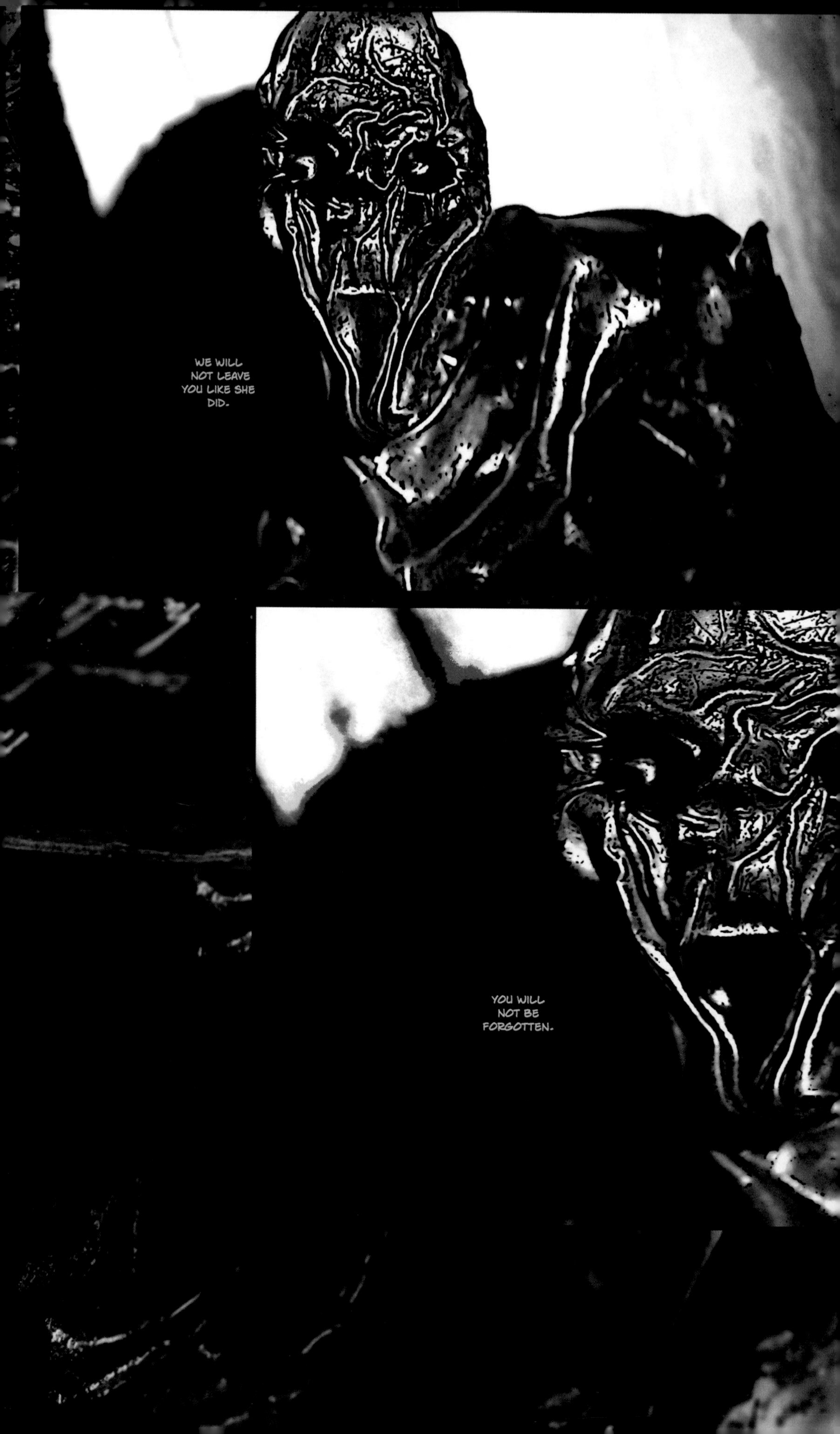
WE WILL NOT LEAVE YOU LIKE SHE DID.
YOU WILL NOT BE FORGOTTEN.

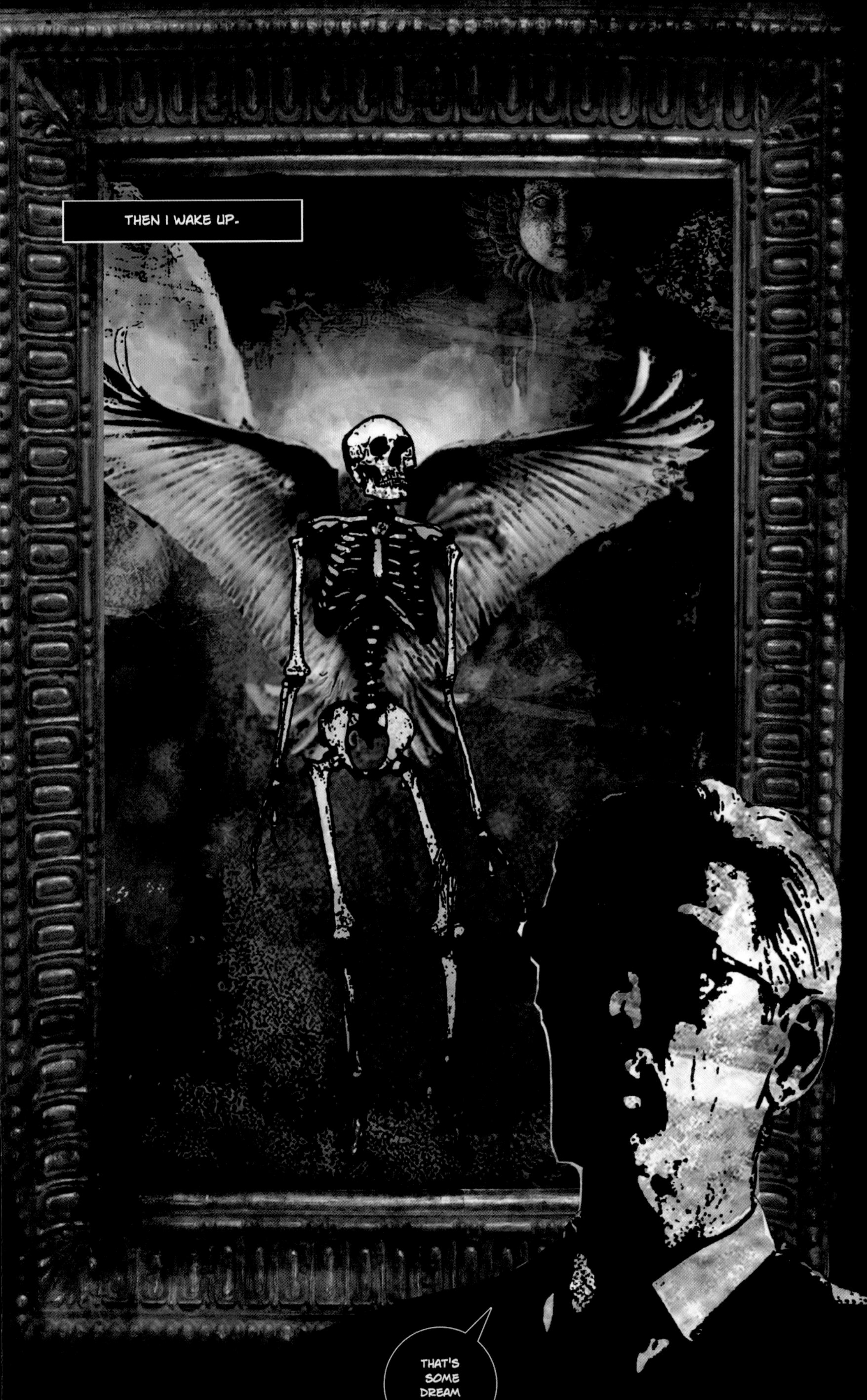
THEN I WAKE UP.
THAT'S SOME DREAM

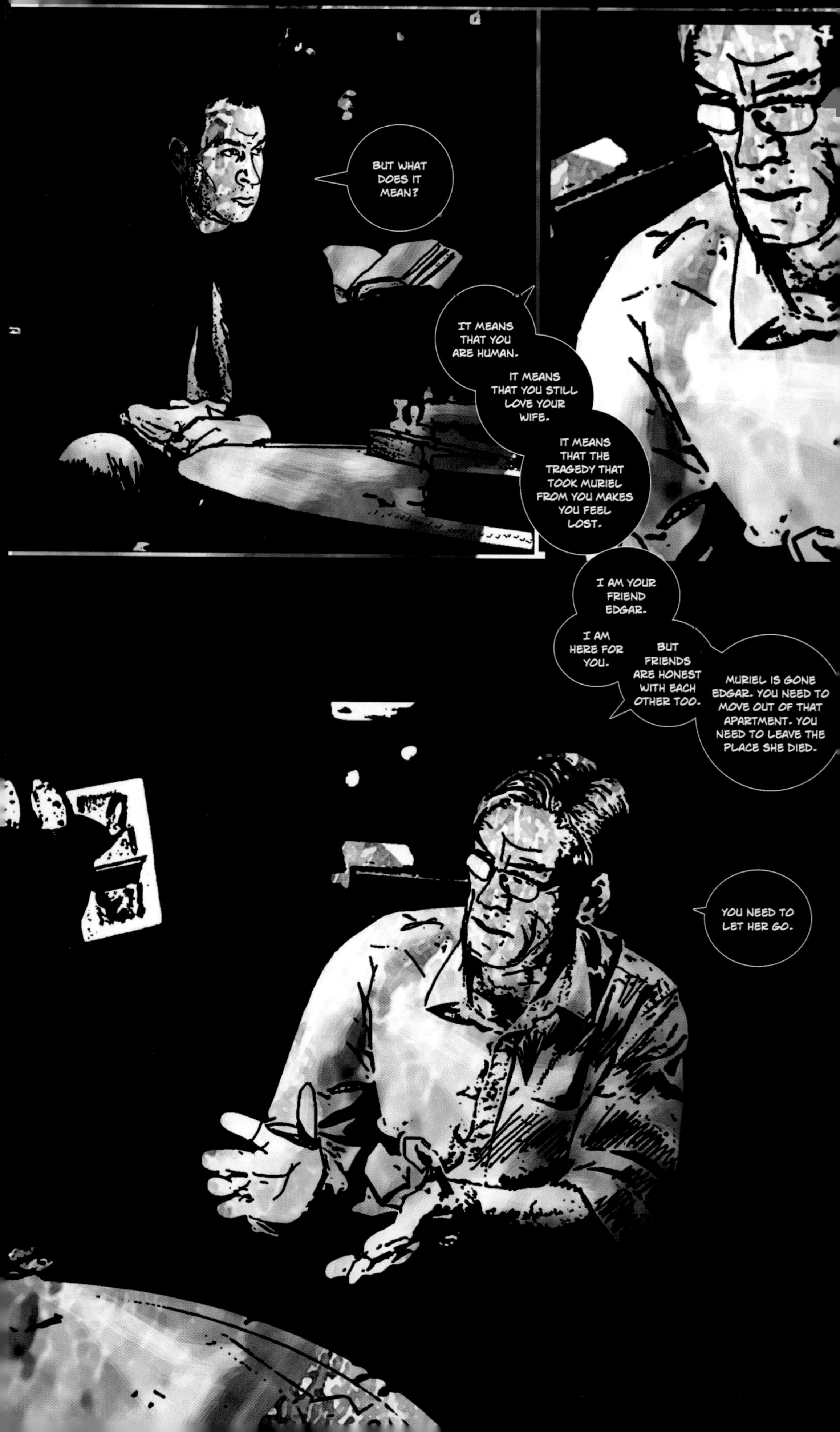
BUT WHAT DOES IT MEAN?
IT MEANS THAT YOU ARE HUMAN.
IT MEANS THAT YOU STILL LOVE YOUR WIFE.
IT MEANS THAT THE TRAGEDY THAT TOOK MURIEL FROM YOU MAKES YOU FEEL LOST.
I AM YOUR FRIEND EDGAR.
I AM HERE FOR YOU.
BUT FRIENDS ARE HONEST WITH EACH OTHER TOO.
MURIEL IS GONE EDGAR. YOU NEED TO MOVE OUT OF THAT APARTMENT. YOU NEED TO LEAVE THE PLACE SHE DIED.
YOU NEED TO LET HER GO.

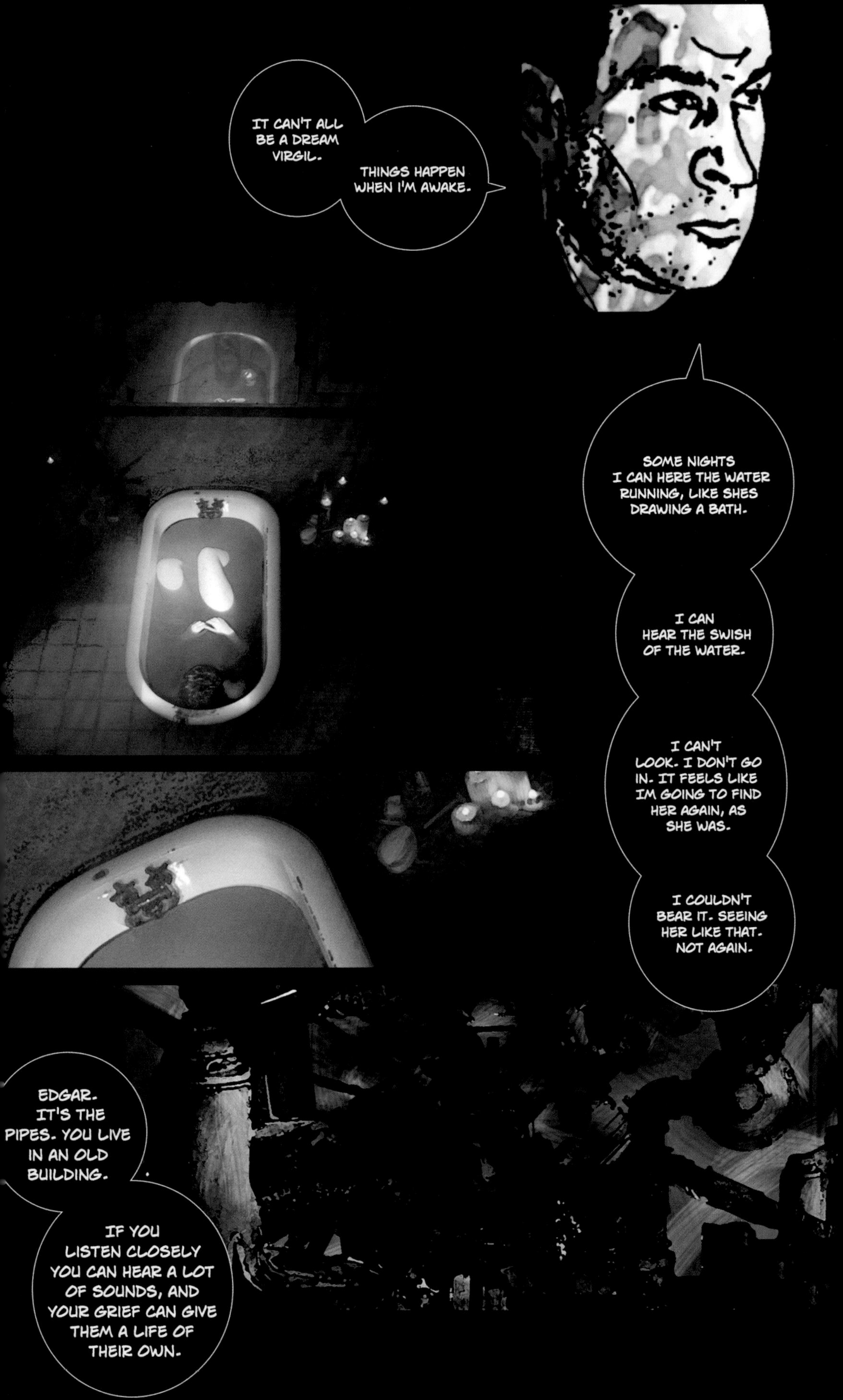
IT CAN'T ALL BE A DREAM VIRGIL.
THINGS HAPPEN WHEN I'M AWAKE.
SOME NIGHTS I CAN HERE THE WATER RUNNING, LIKE SHES DRAWING A BATH.
I CAN HEAR THE SWISH OF THE WATER.
I CAN'T LOOK. I DON'T GO IN. IT FEELS LIKE IM GOING TO FIND HER AGAIN, AS SHE WAS.
I COULDN'T BEAR IT. SEEING HER LIKE THAT. NOT AGAIN.
EDGAR. IT'S THE PIPES. YOU LIVE IN AN OLD BUILDING.
IF YOU LISTEN CLOSELY YOU CAN HEAR A LOT OF SOUNDS, AND YOUR GRIEF CAN GIVE THEM A LIFE OF THEIR OWN.

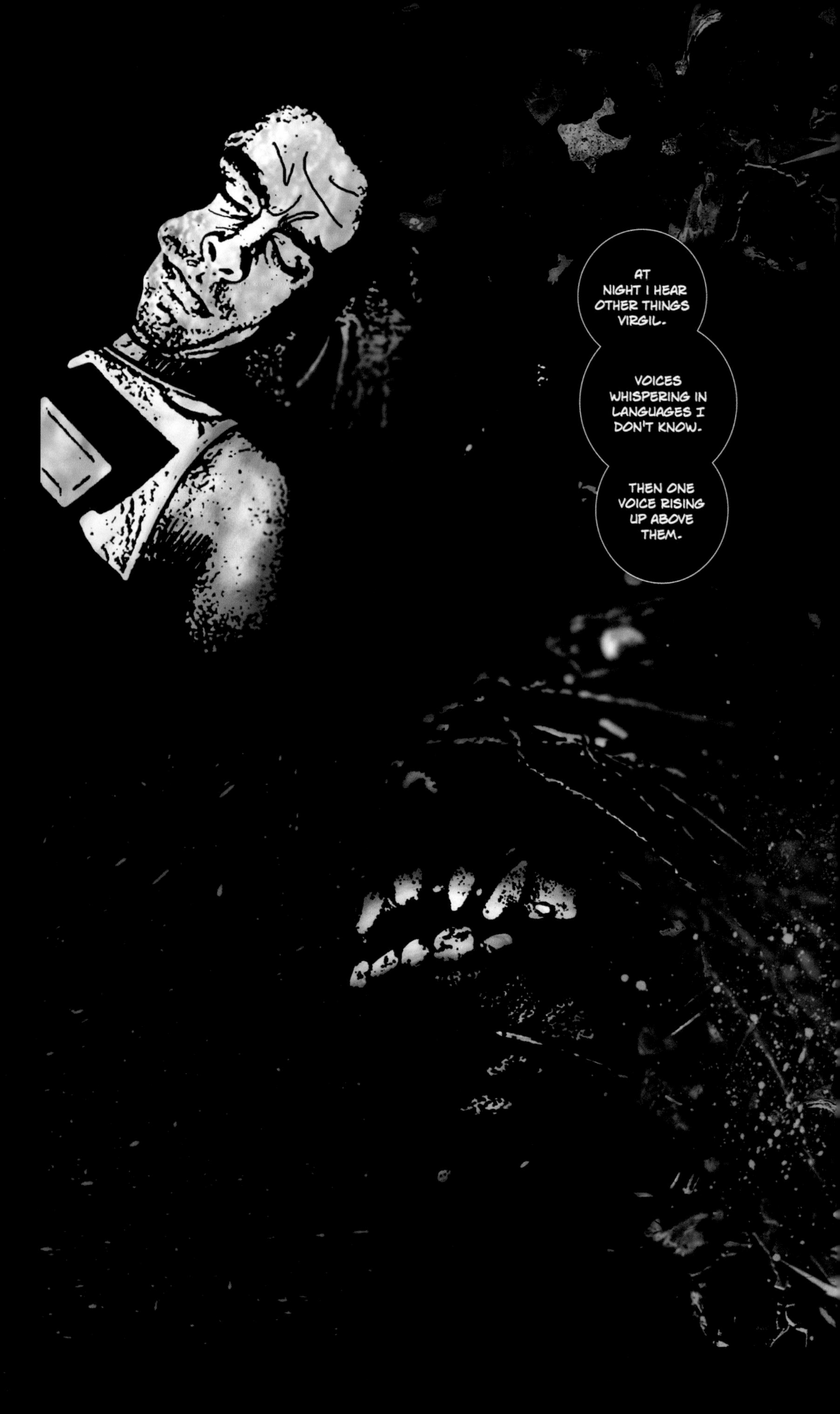
AT NIGHT I HEAR OTHER THINGS VIRGIL.
VOICES WHISPERING IN LANGUAGES I DON'T KNOW.
THEN ONE VOICE RISING UP ABOVE THEM.

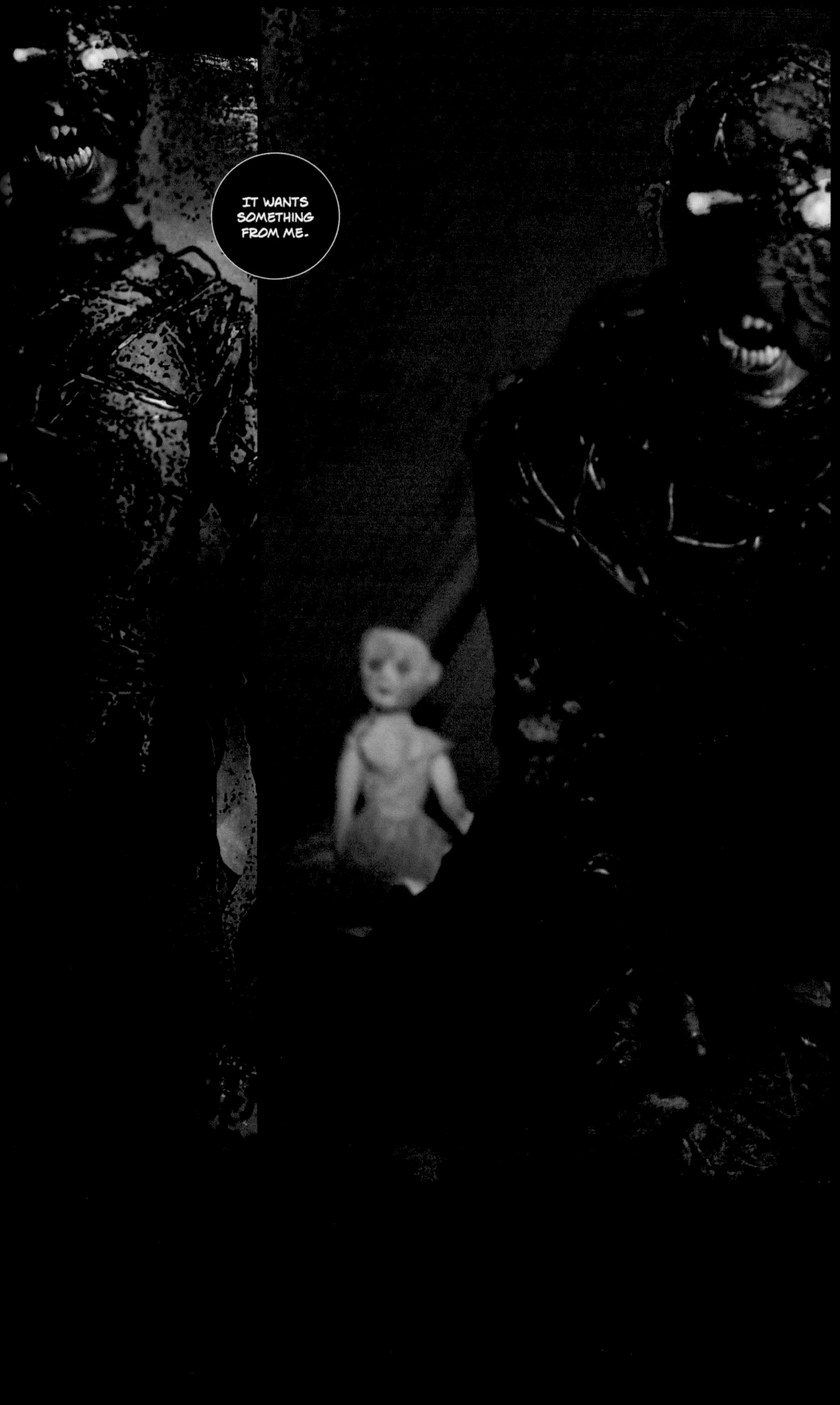
IT WANTS SOMETHING FROM ME.

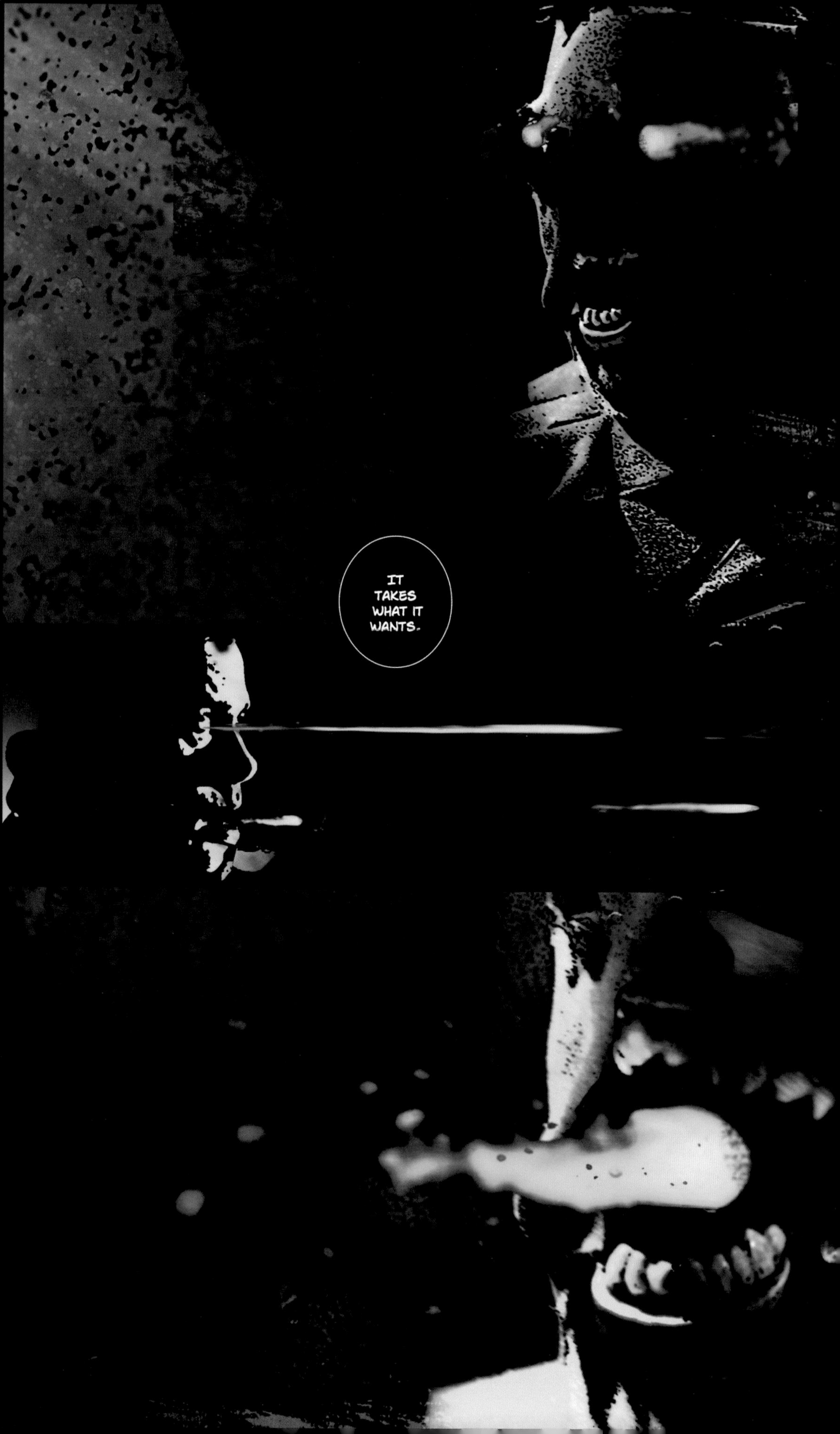
IT TAKES WHAT IT WANTS.

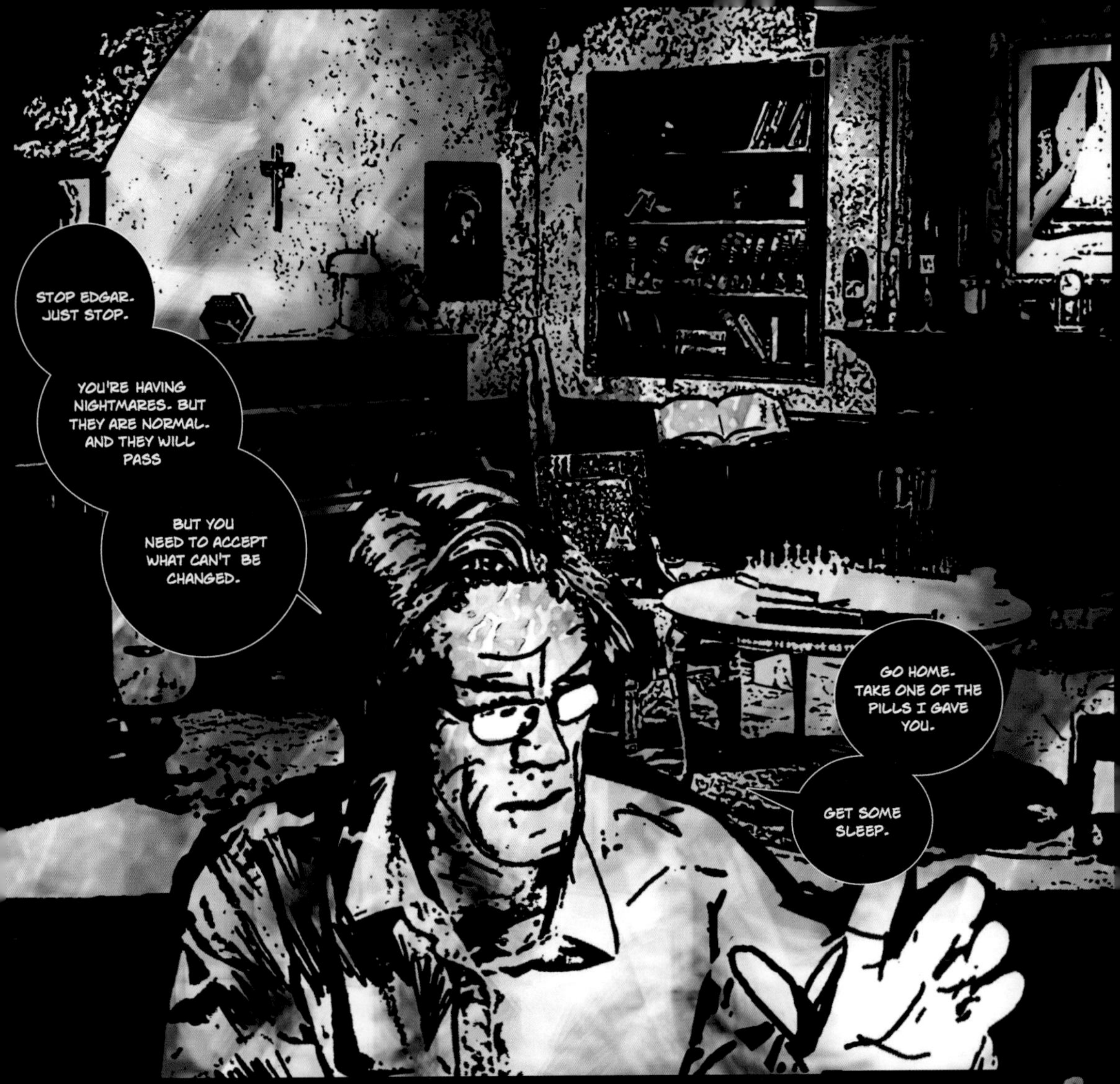
STOP EDGAR. JUST STOP.
YOU'RE HAVING NIGHTMARES. BUT THEY ARE NORMAL. AND THEY WILL PASS
BUT YOU NEED TO ACCEPT WHAT CAN'T BE CHANGED.
GO HOME. TAKE ONE OF THE PILLS I GAVE YOU.
GET SOME SLEEP.

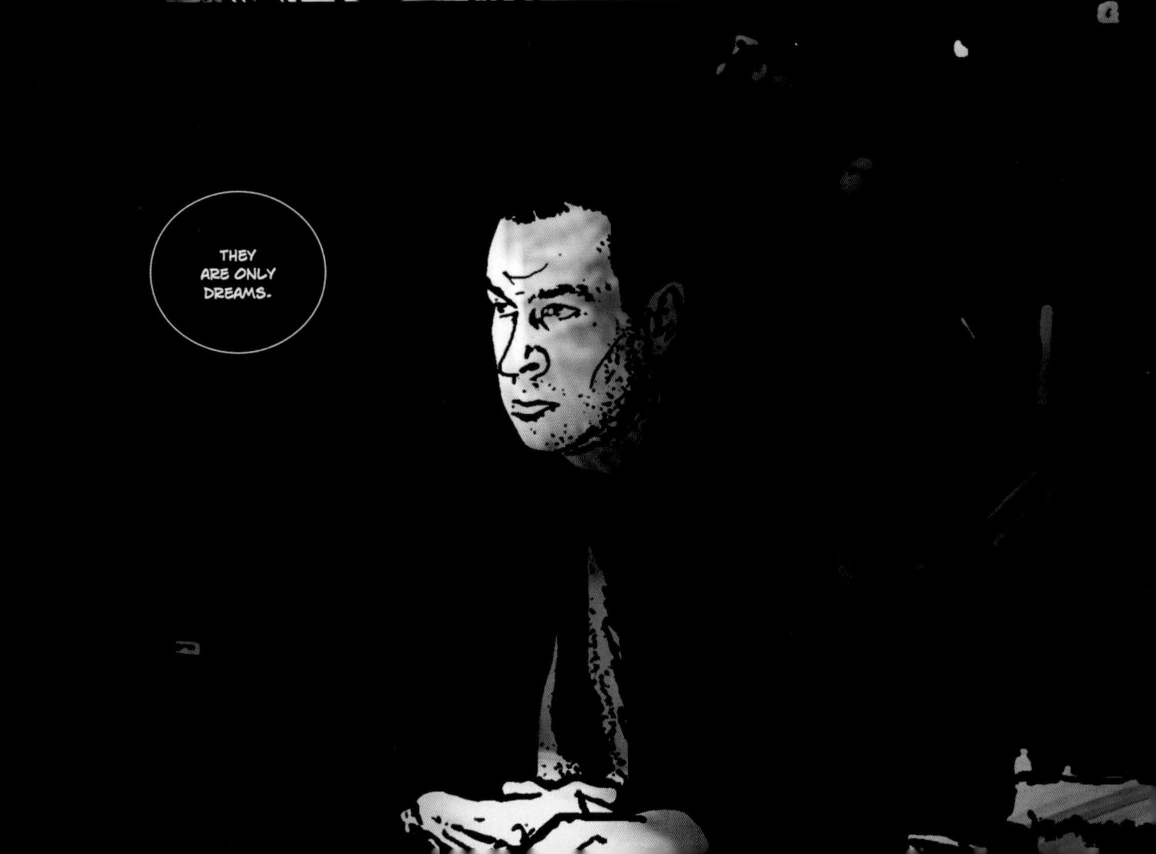
THEY ARE ONLY DREAMS.

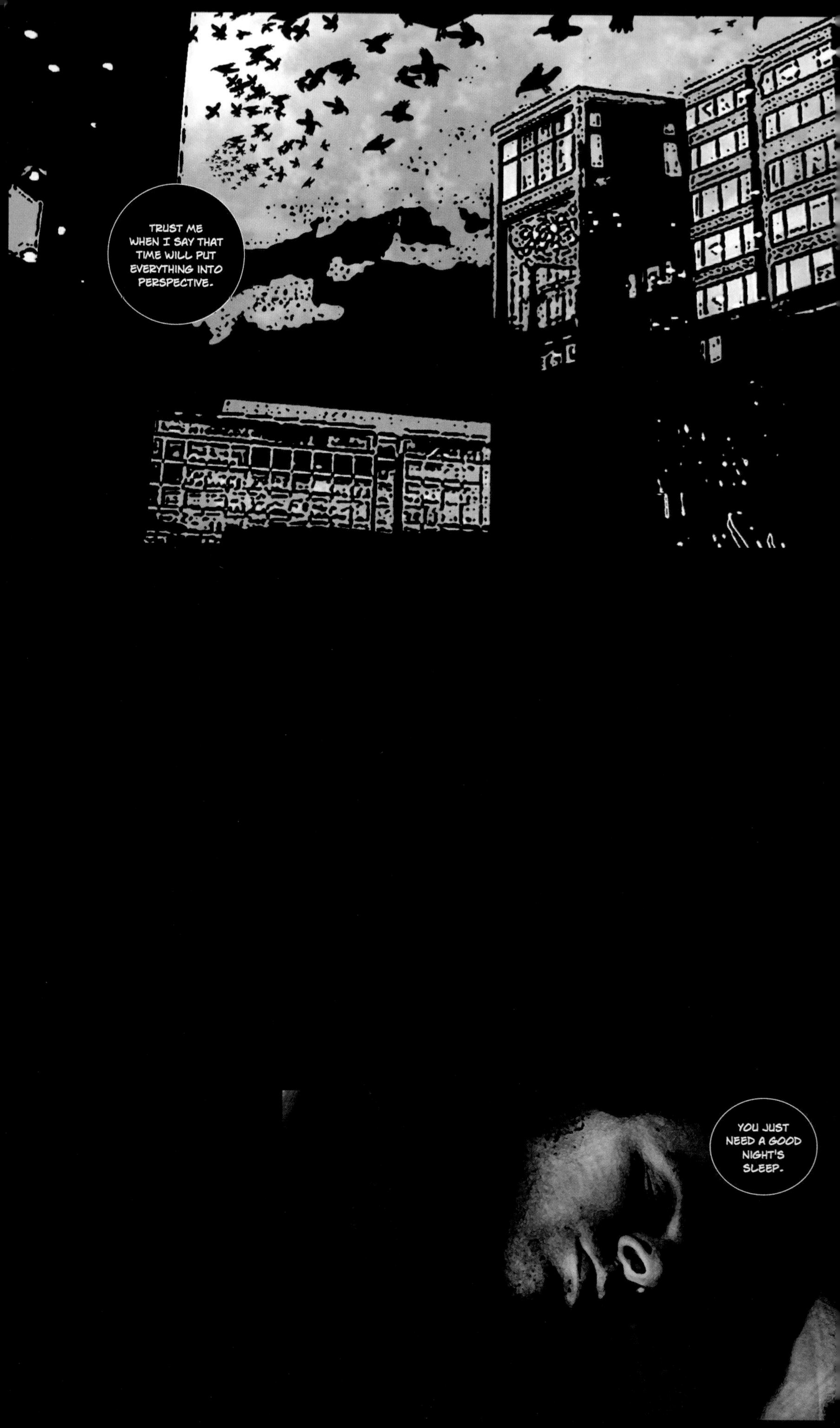
TRUST ME WHEN I SAY THAT TIME WILL PUT EVERYTHING INTO PERSPECTIVE.
YOU JUST NEED A GOOD NIGHT'S SLEEP.

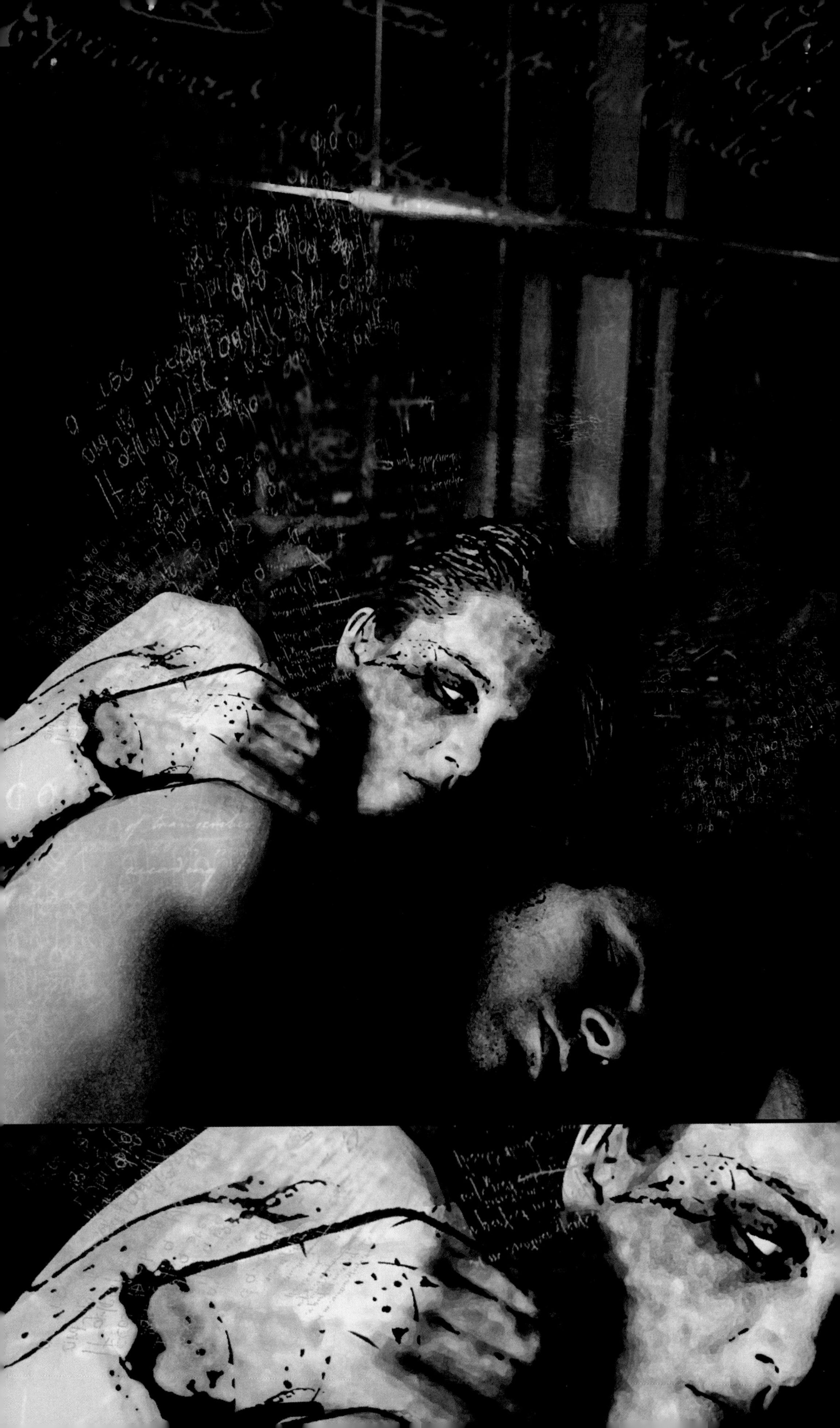

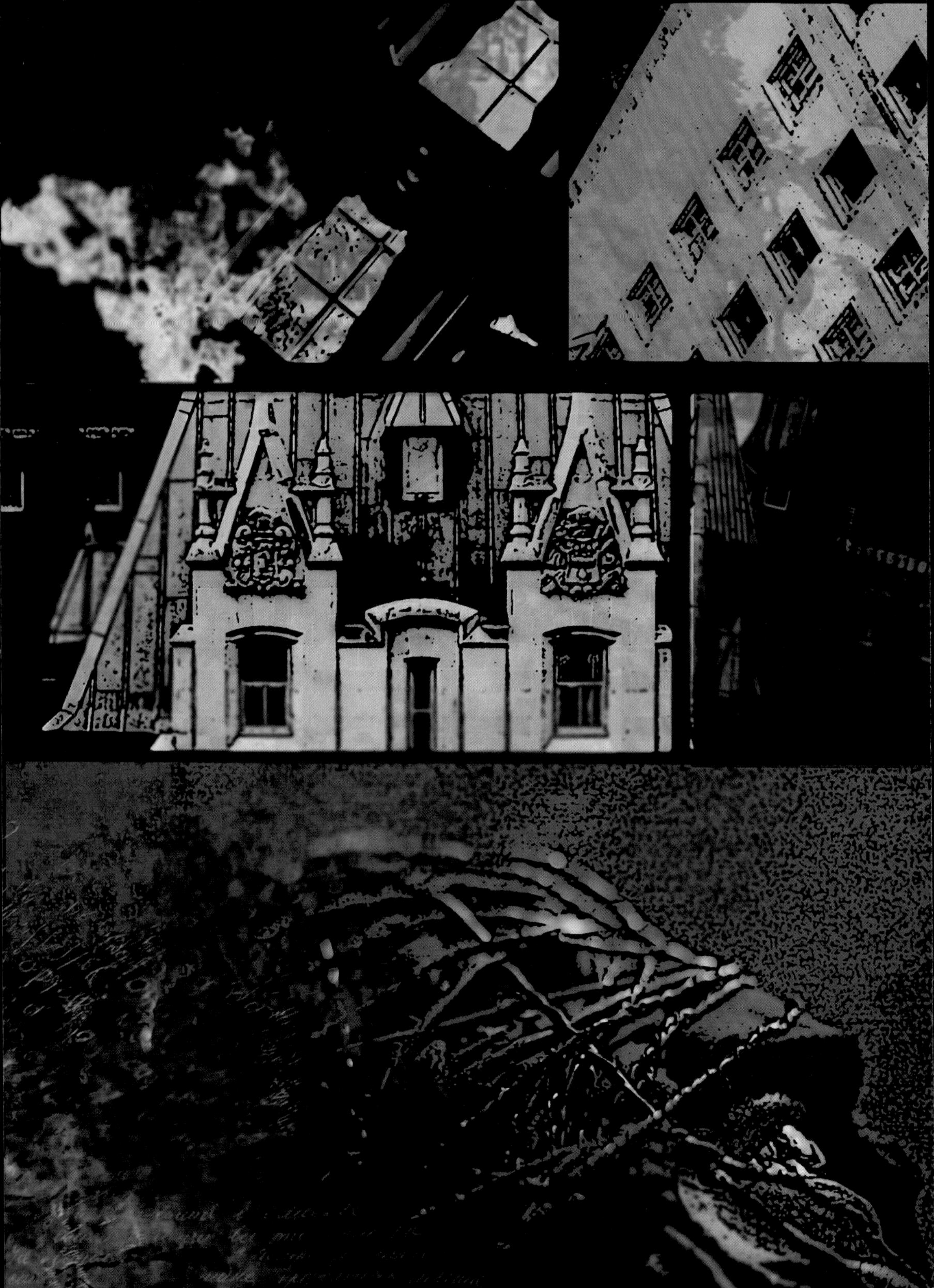

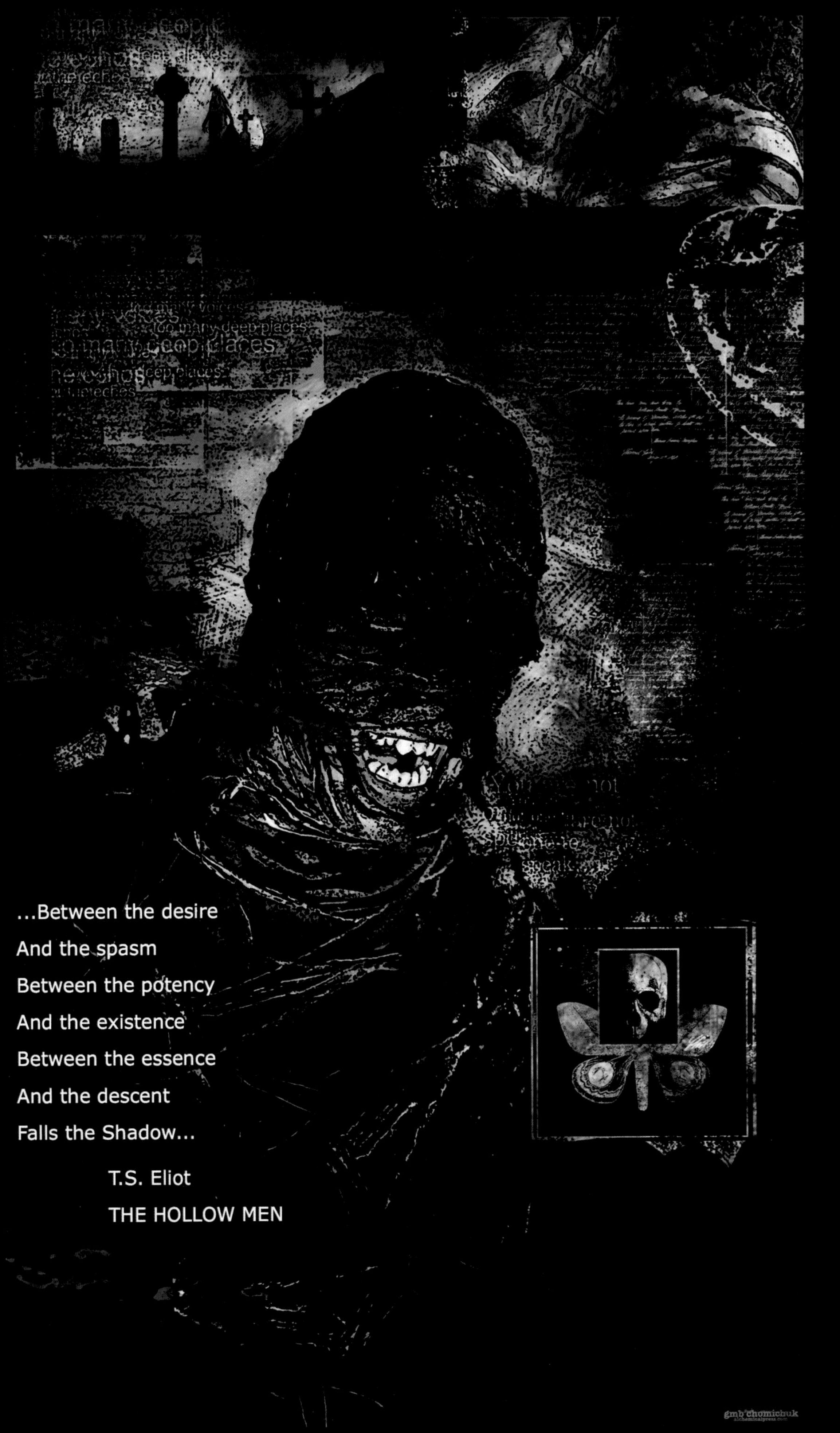
...Between the desire
And the spasm
Between the potency
And the existence
Between the essence
And the descent
Falls the Shadow...
T.S. Eliot
THE HOLLOW MEN
gmb chomichuk

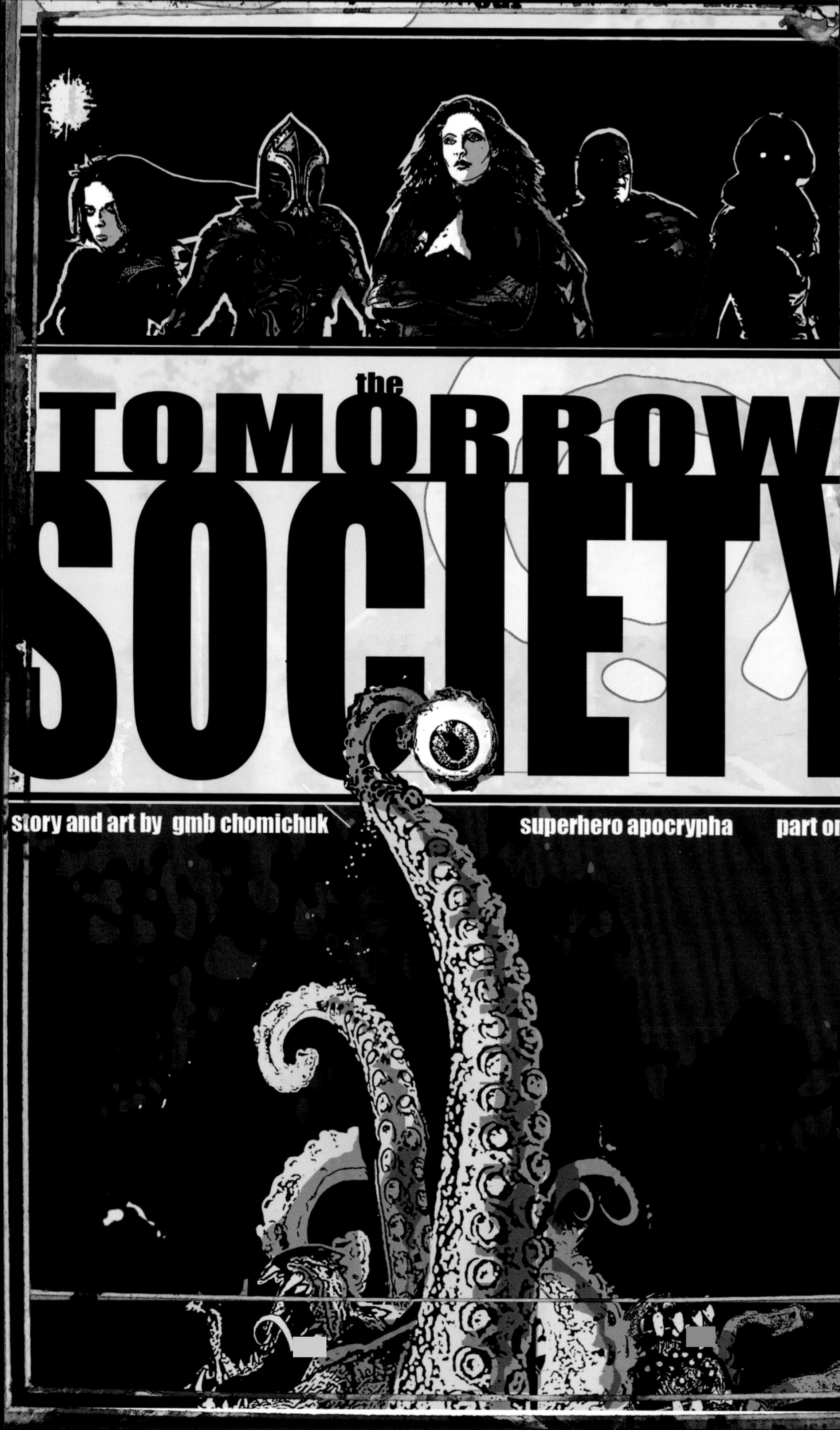
the
TOMORROW
SOCIETY
story and art by gmb chomichuk
superhero apocrypha
part on

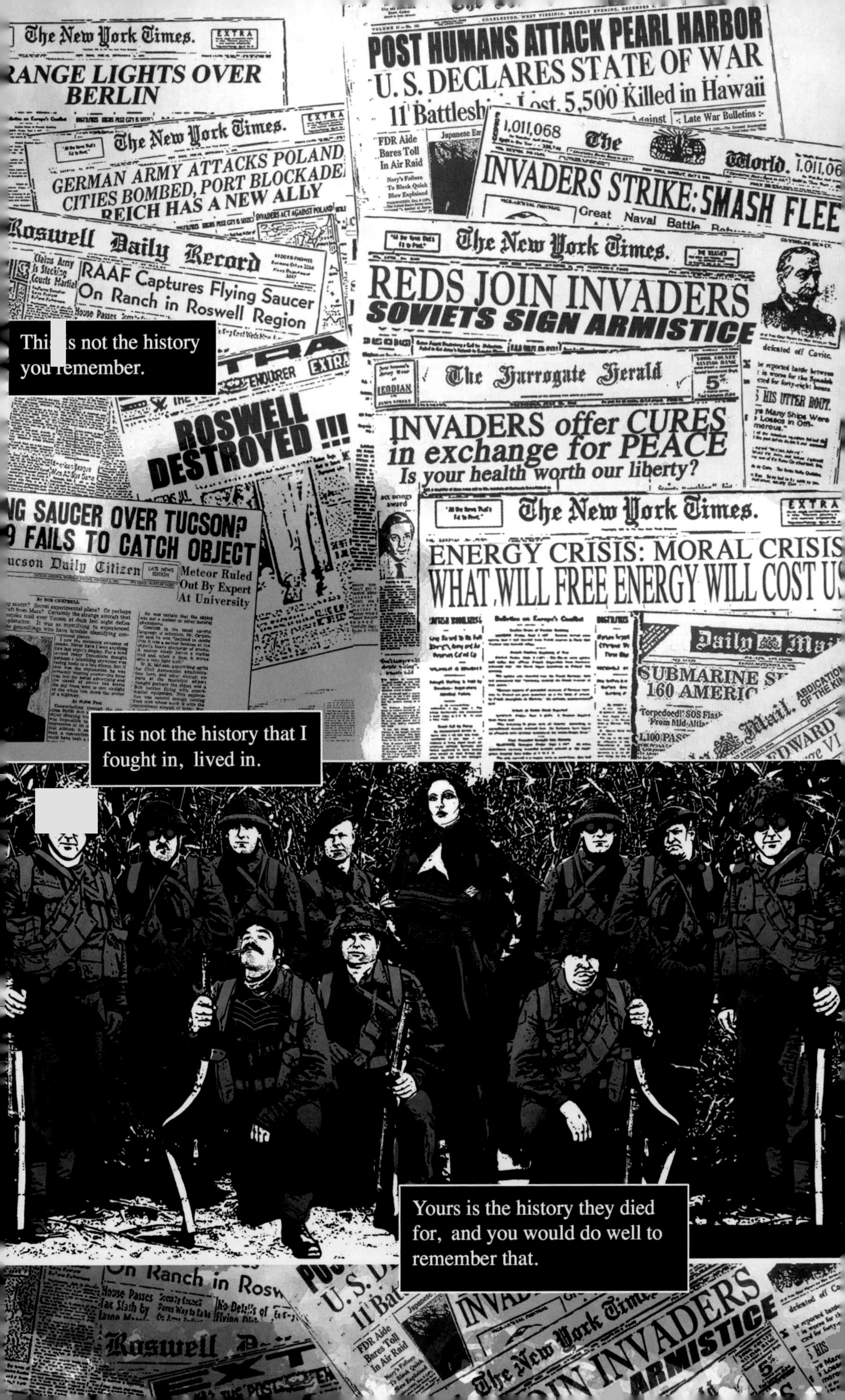
The New York Times.
RANGE LIGHTS OVER BERLIN
POST HUMANS ATTACK PEARL HARBOR
U.S. DECLARES STATE OF WAR
5,500 Killed in Hawaii
The New York Times.
GERMAN ARMY ATTACKS POLAND
CITIES BOMBED, PORT BLOCKADED
REICH HAS A NEW ALLY
The World.
INVADERS STRIKE: SMASH FLEE
Great Naval Battle
Roswell Daily Record
RAAF Captures Flying Saucer On Ranch in Roswell Region
The New York Times.
REDS JOIN INVADERS
SOVIETS SIGN ARMISTICE
This is not the history you remember.
The Harrogate Herald
INVADERS offer CURES in exchange for PEACE
Is your health worth our liberty?
ROSWELL DESTROYED !!!
NG SAUCER OVER TUCSON?
9 FAILS TO CATCH OBJECT
Tucson Daily Citizen
Meteor Ruled Out By Expert At University
The New York Times.
ENERGY CRISIS: MORAL CRISIS
WHAT WILL FREE ENERGY WILL COST US
Daily Mail
SUBMARINE S
160 AMERIC
It is not the history that I fought in, lived in.
Yours is the history they died for, and you would do well to remember that.

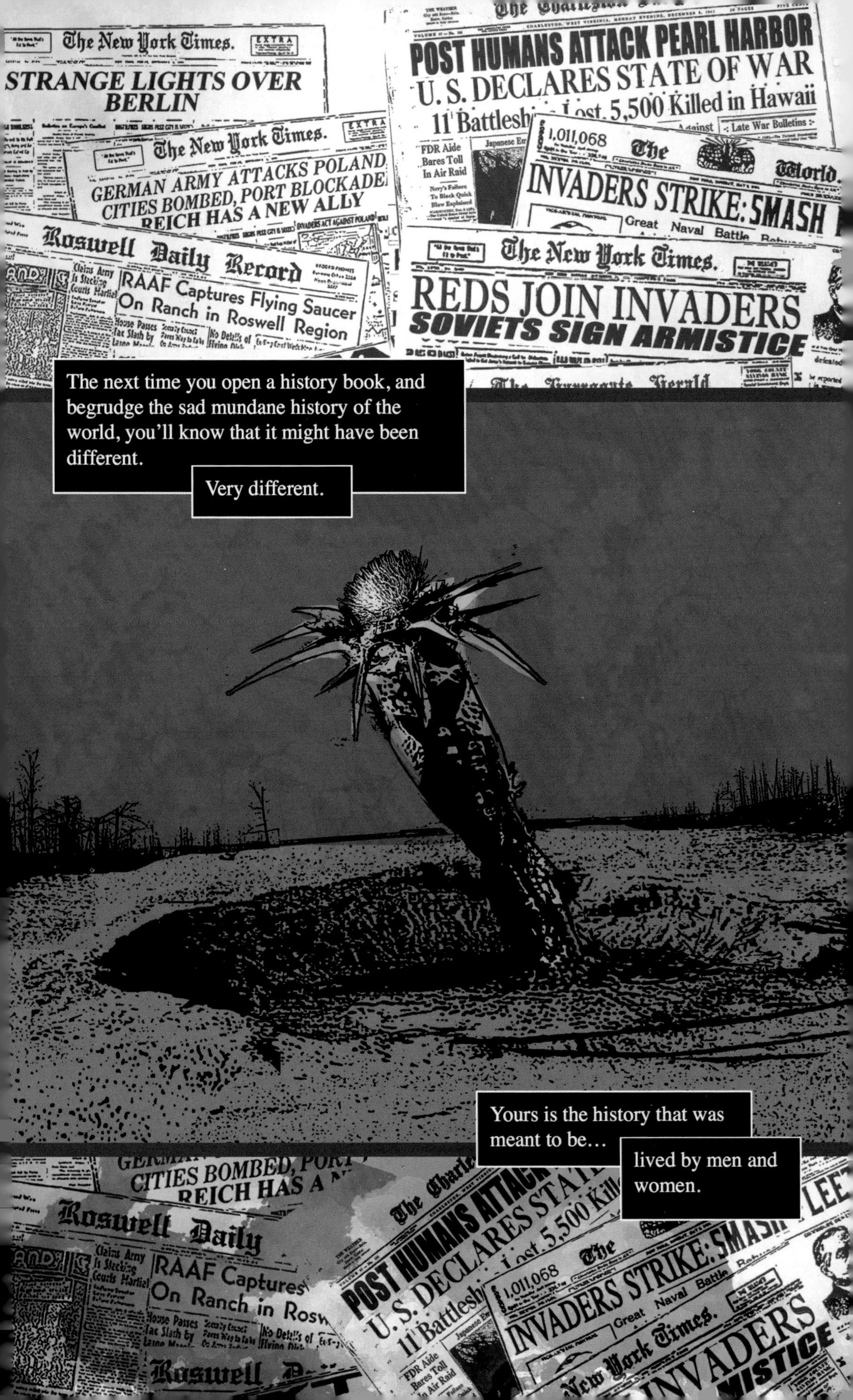

The New York Times.
STRANGE LIGHTS OVER BERLIN
POST HUMANS ATTACK PEARL HARBOR
U.S. DECLARES STATE OF WAR
The New York Times.
GERMAN ARMY ATTACKS POLAND
CITIES BOMBED, PORT BLOCKADE
REICH HAS A NEW ALLY
The World.
INVADERS STRIKE: SMASH
Roswell Daily Record
RAAF Captures Flying Saucer On Ranch in Roswell Region
The New York Times.
REDS JOIN INVADERS
SOVIETS SIGN ARMISTICE
The next time you open a history book, and begrudge the sad mundane history of the world, you'll know that it might have been different.
Very different.
Yours is the history that was meant to be…
lived by men and women.

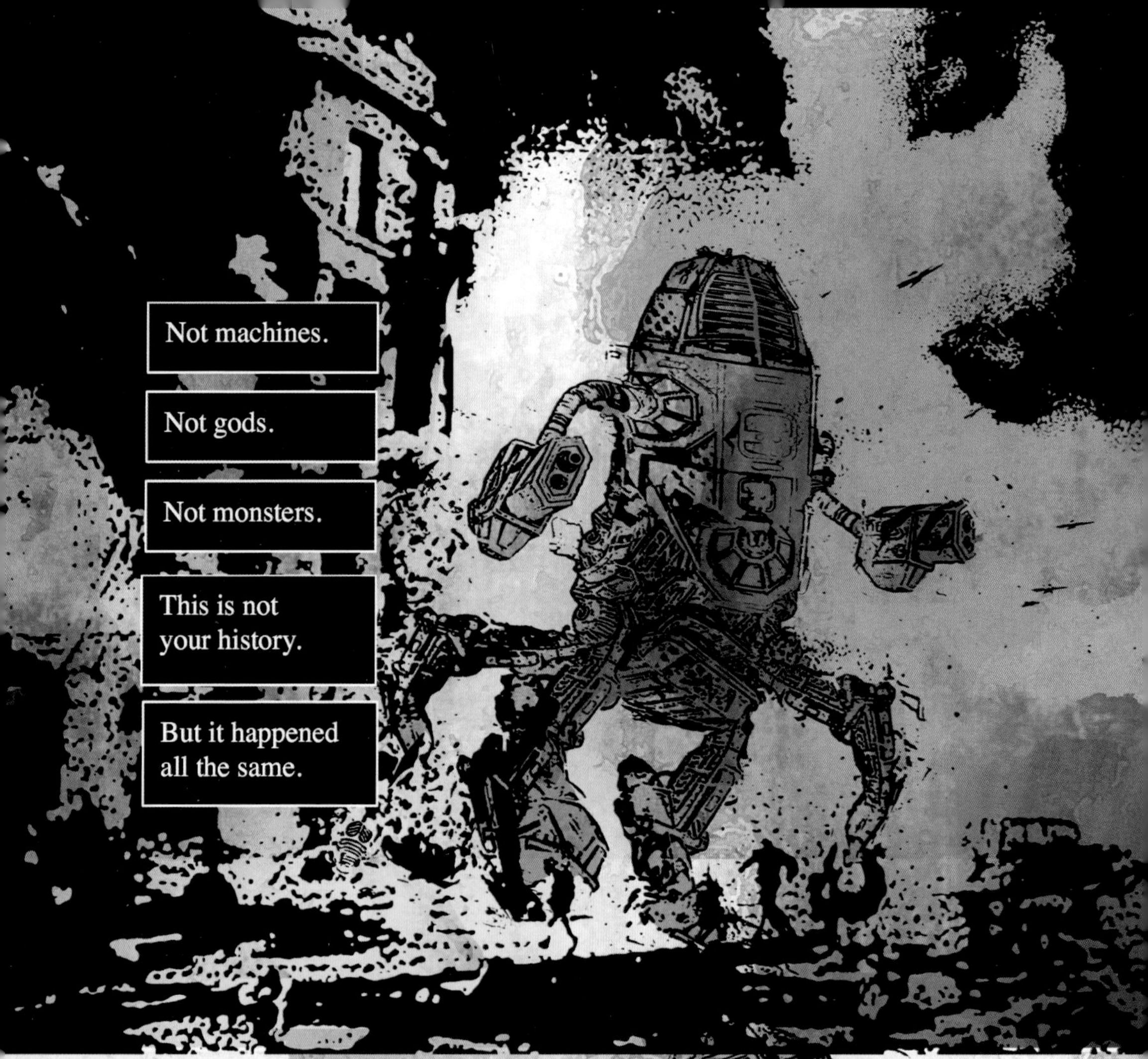
Not machines.
Not gods.
Not monsters.
This is not your history.
But it happened all the same.
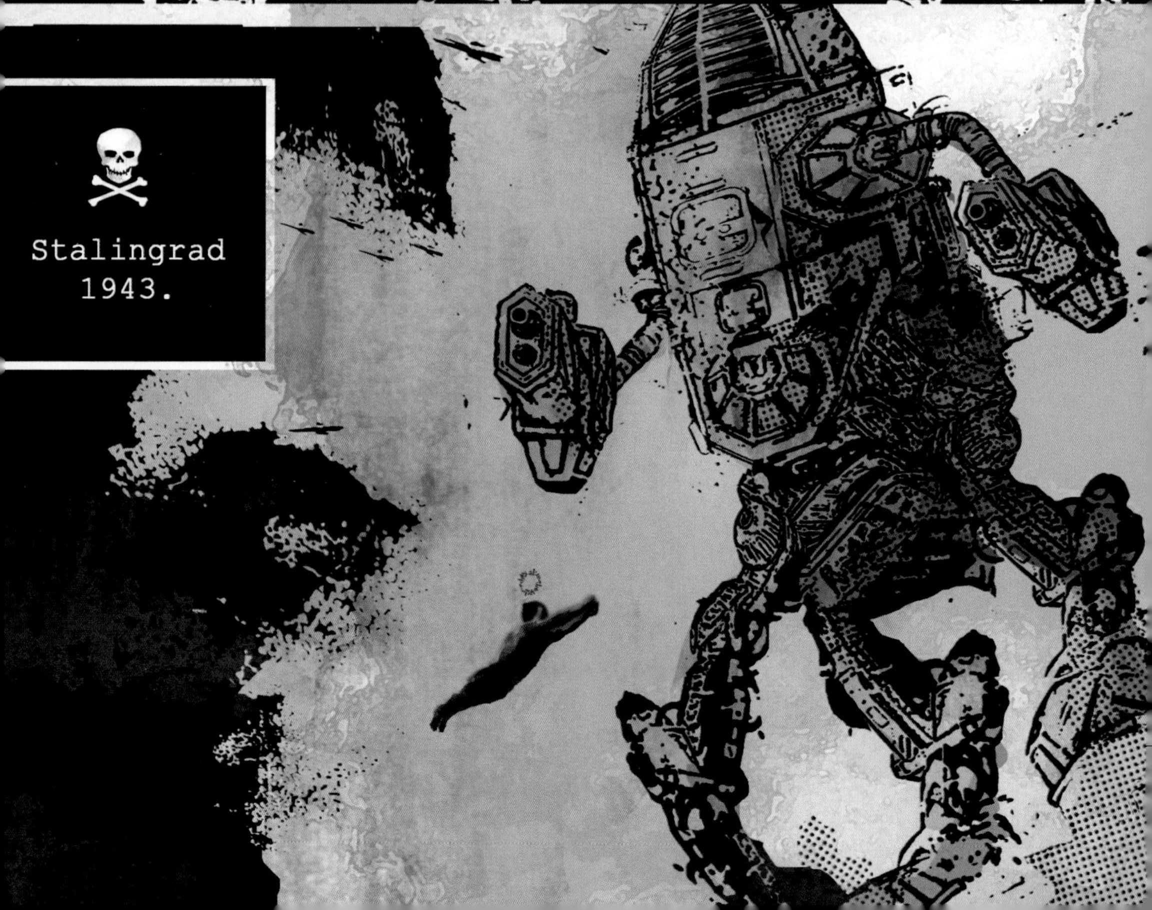
Stalingrad 1943.

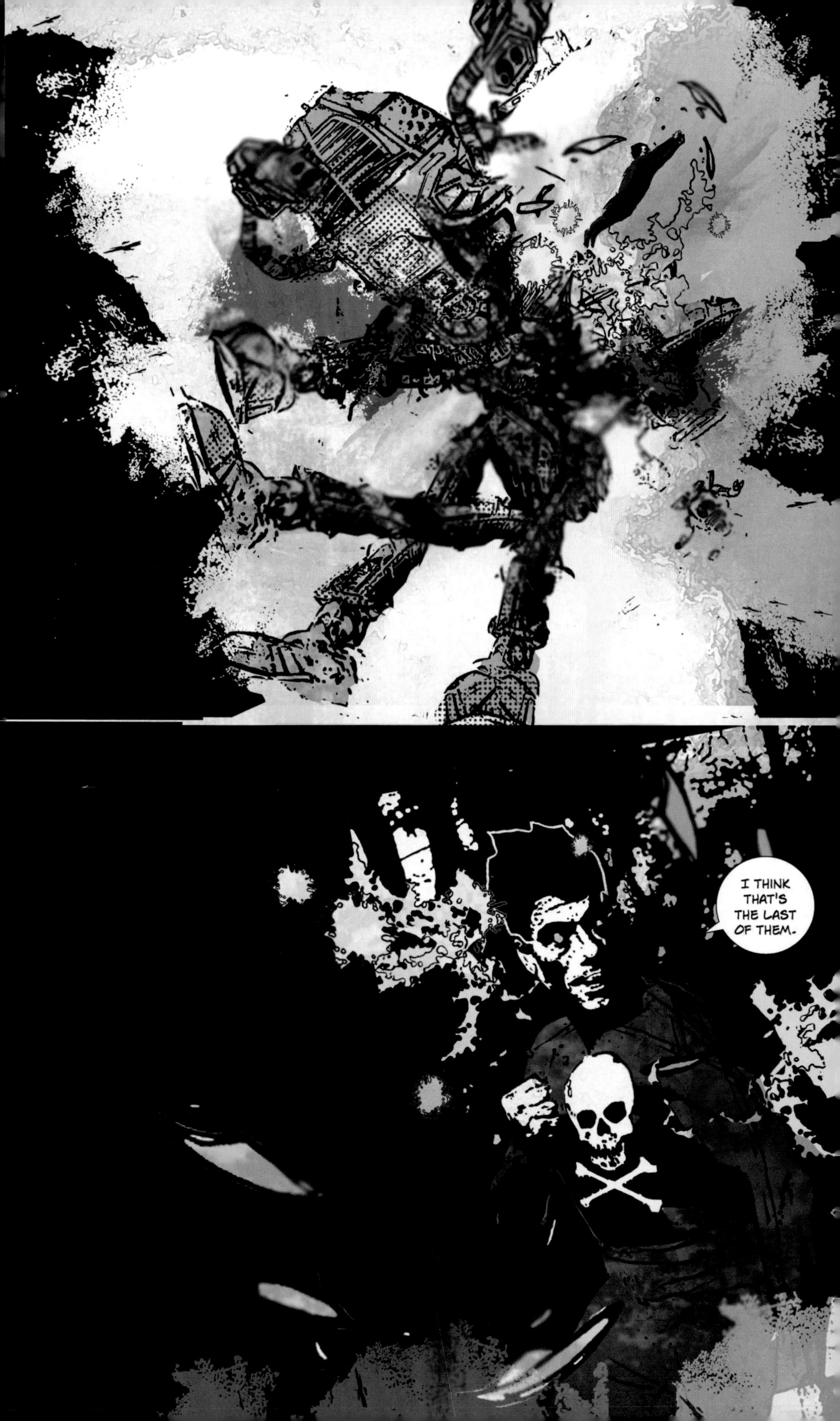
I THINK THAT'S THE LAST OF THEM.

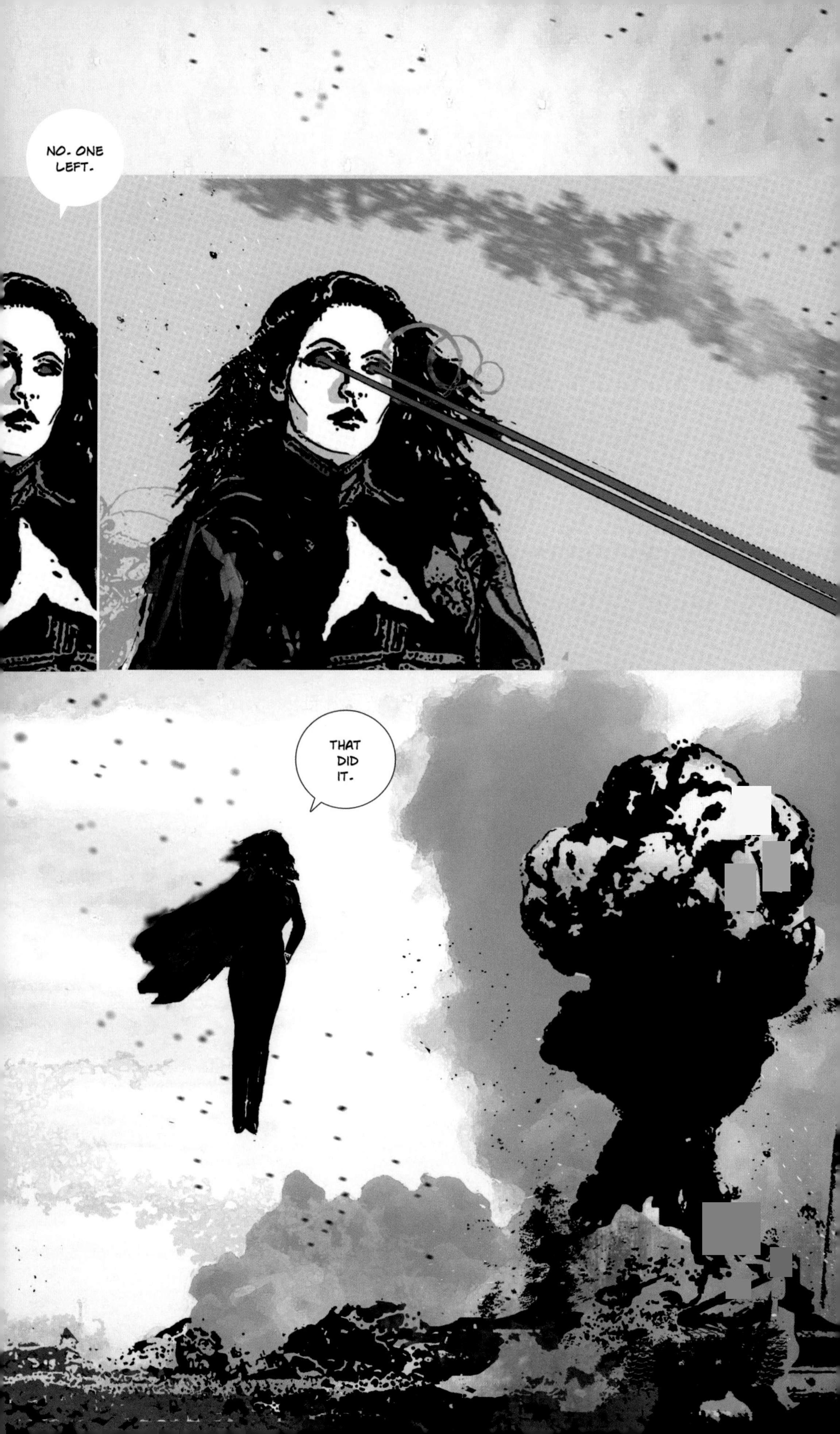
NO. ONE LEFT.
THAT DID IT.

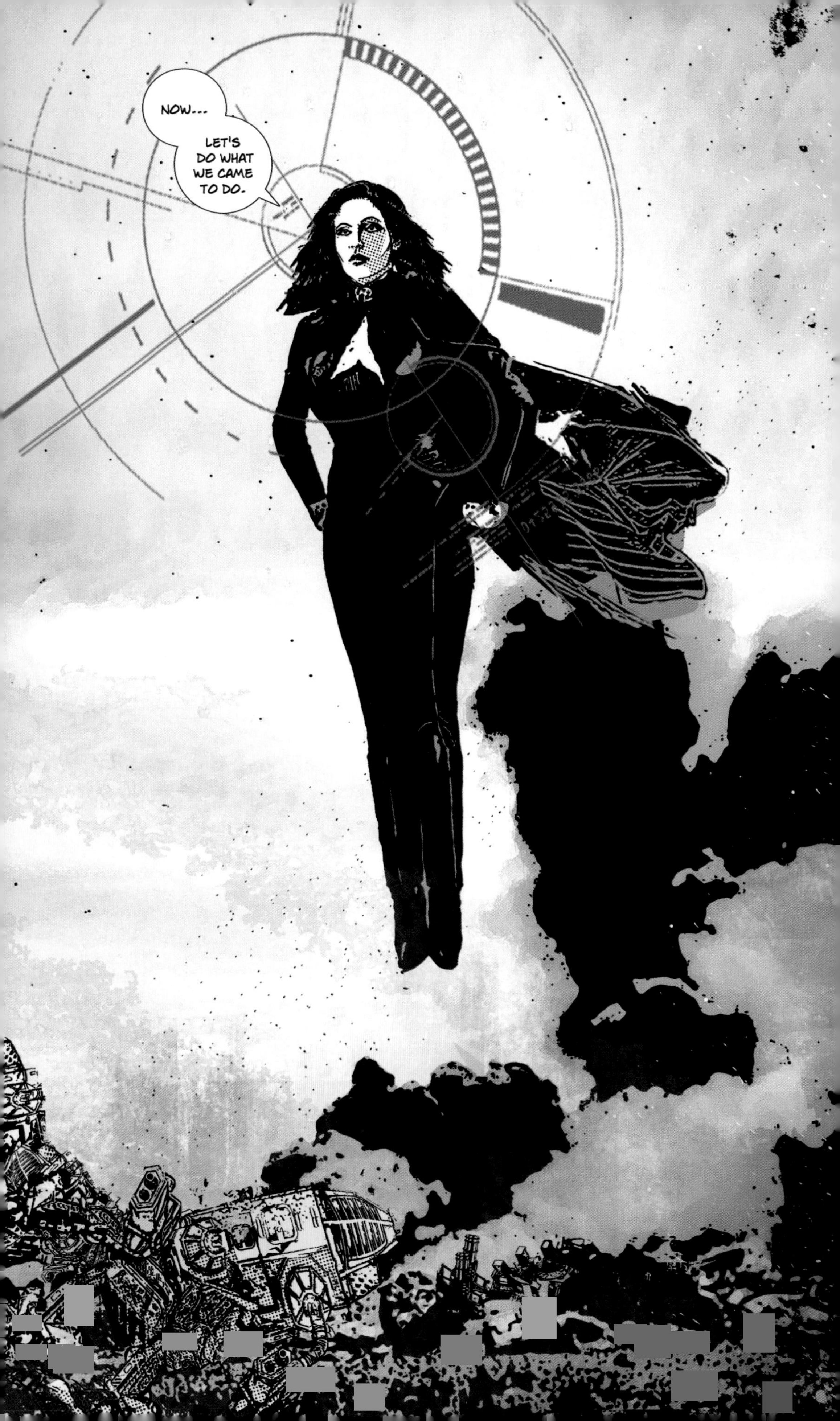
NOW...
LET'S DO WHAT WE CAME TO DO.

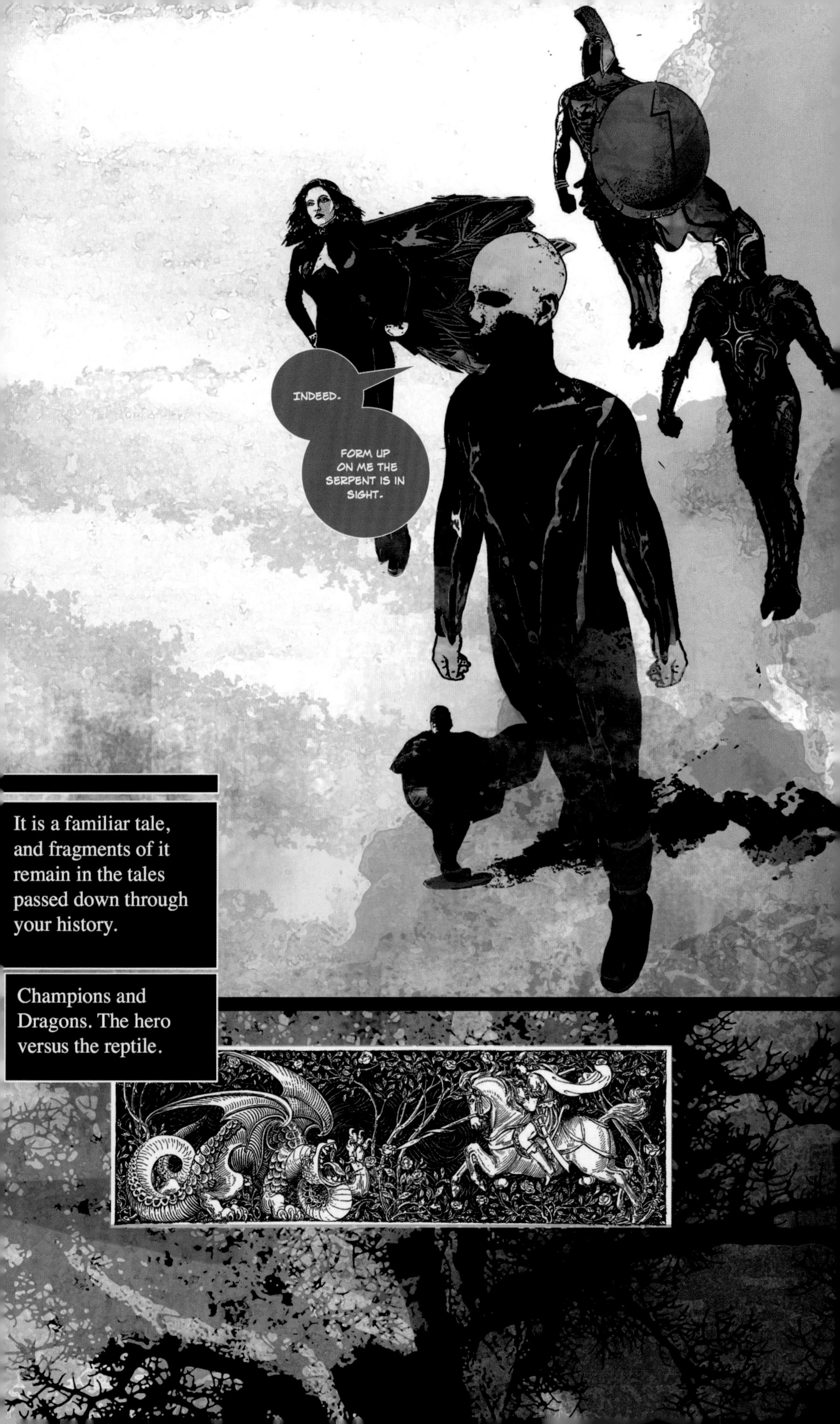
INDEED.
FORM UP ON ME THE SERPENT IS IN SIGHT.
It is a familiar tale, and fragments of it remain in the tales passed down through your history.
Champions and Dragons. The hero versus the reptile.

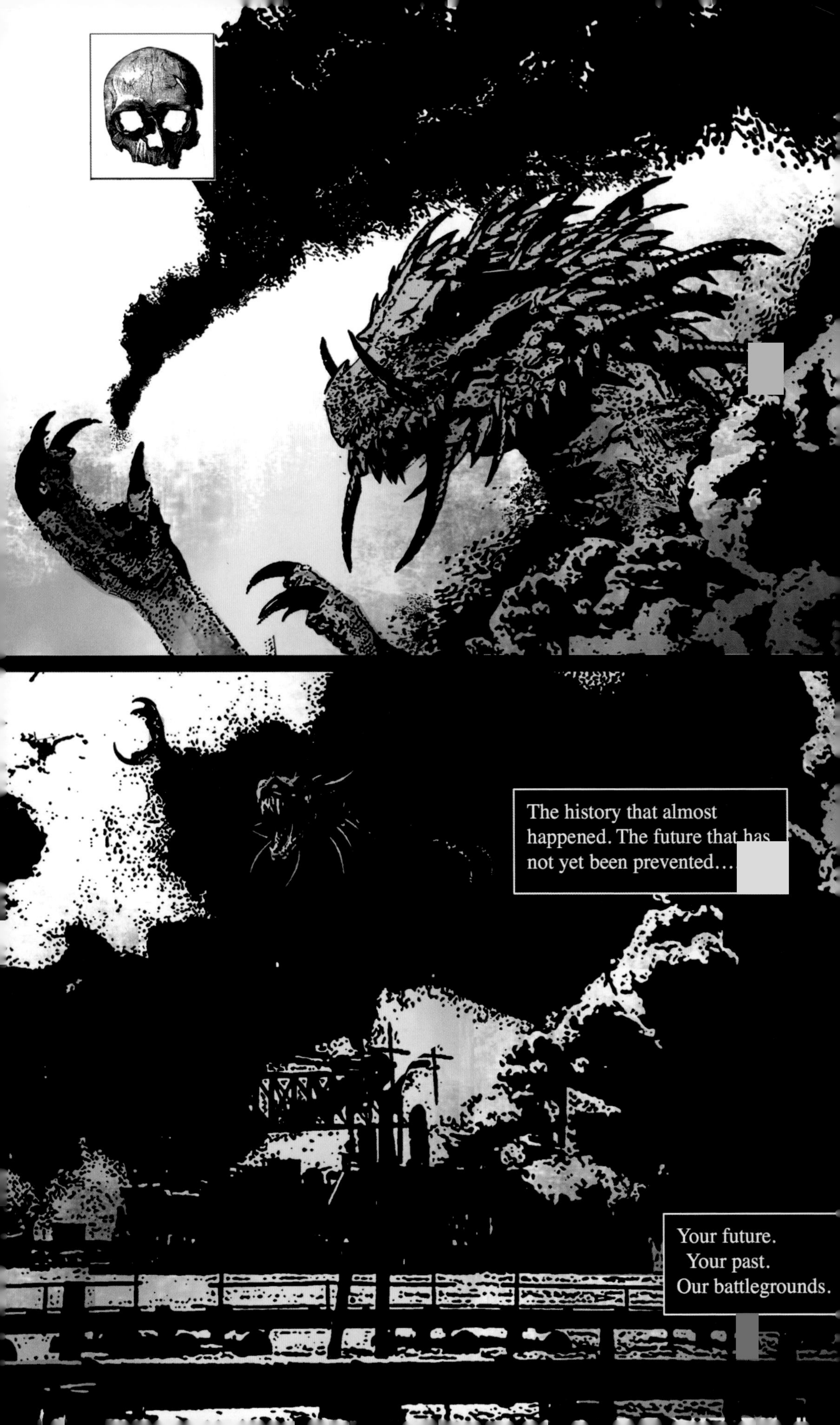
The history that almost happened. The future that has not yet been prevented…
Your future. Your past. Our battlegrounds.

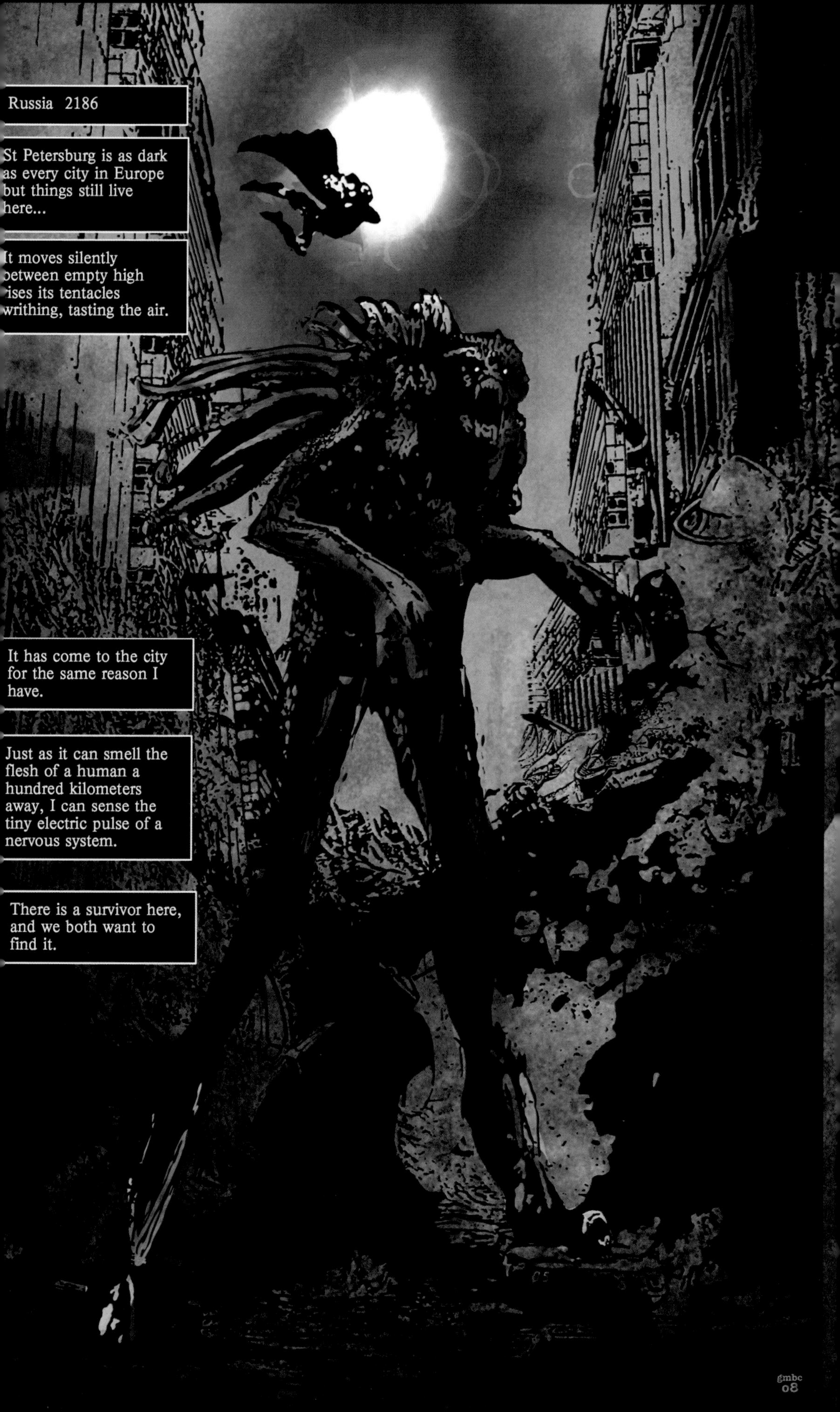
Russia 2186
St Petersburg is as dark as every city in Europe but things still live here...
It moves silently between empty high rises its tentacles writhing, tasting the air.
It has come to the city for the same reason I have.
Just as it can smell the flesh of a human a hundred kilometers away, I can sense the tiny electric pulse of a nervous system.
There is a survivor here, and we both want to find it.

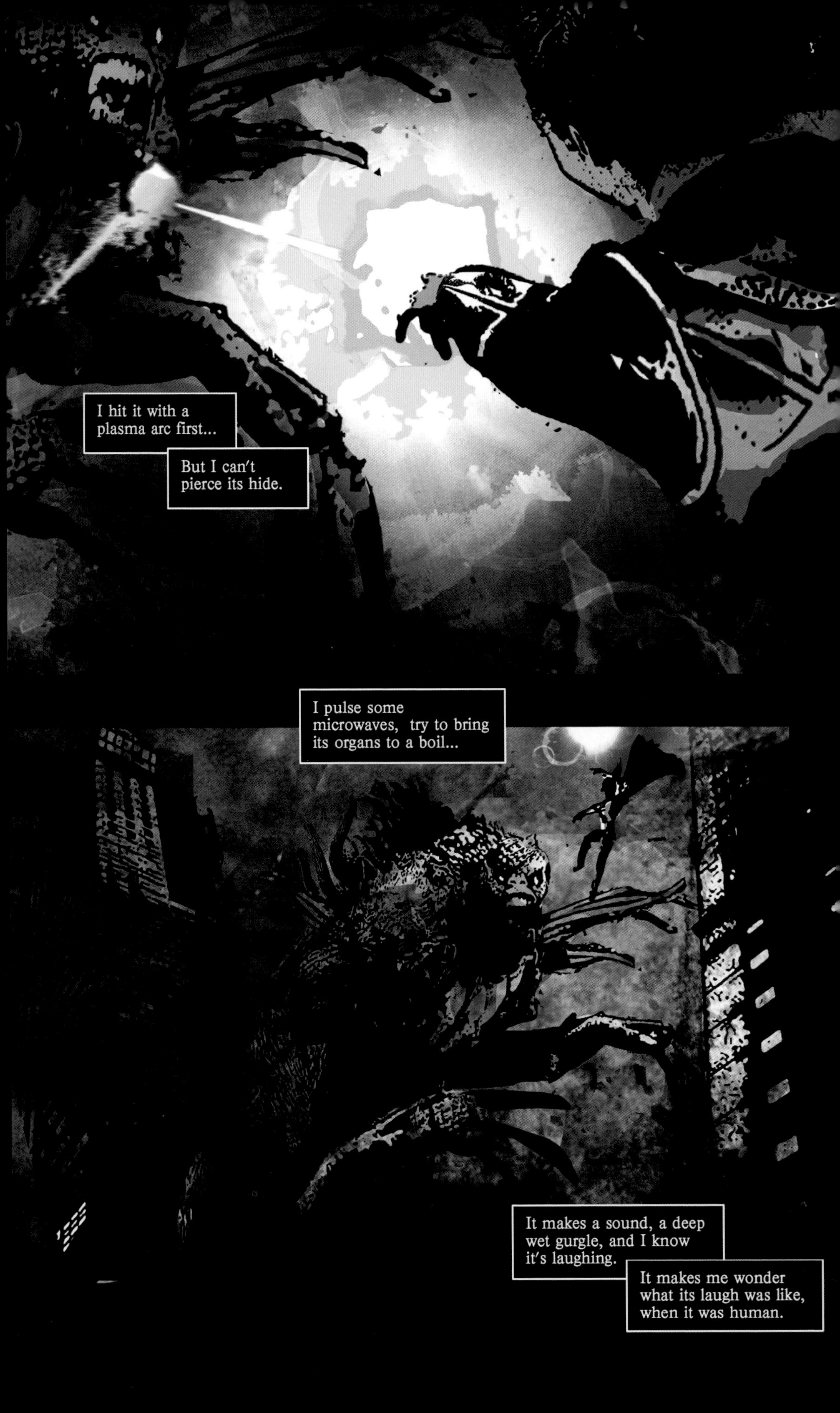
I hit it with a plasma arc first...
But I can't pierce its hide.
I pulse some microwaves, try to bring its organs to a boil...
It makes a sound, a deep wet gurgle, and I know it's laughing.
It makes me wonder what its laugh was like, when it was human.

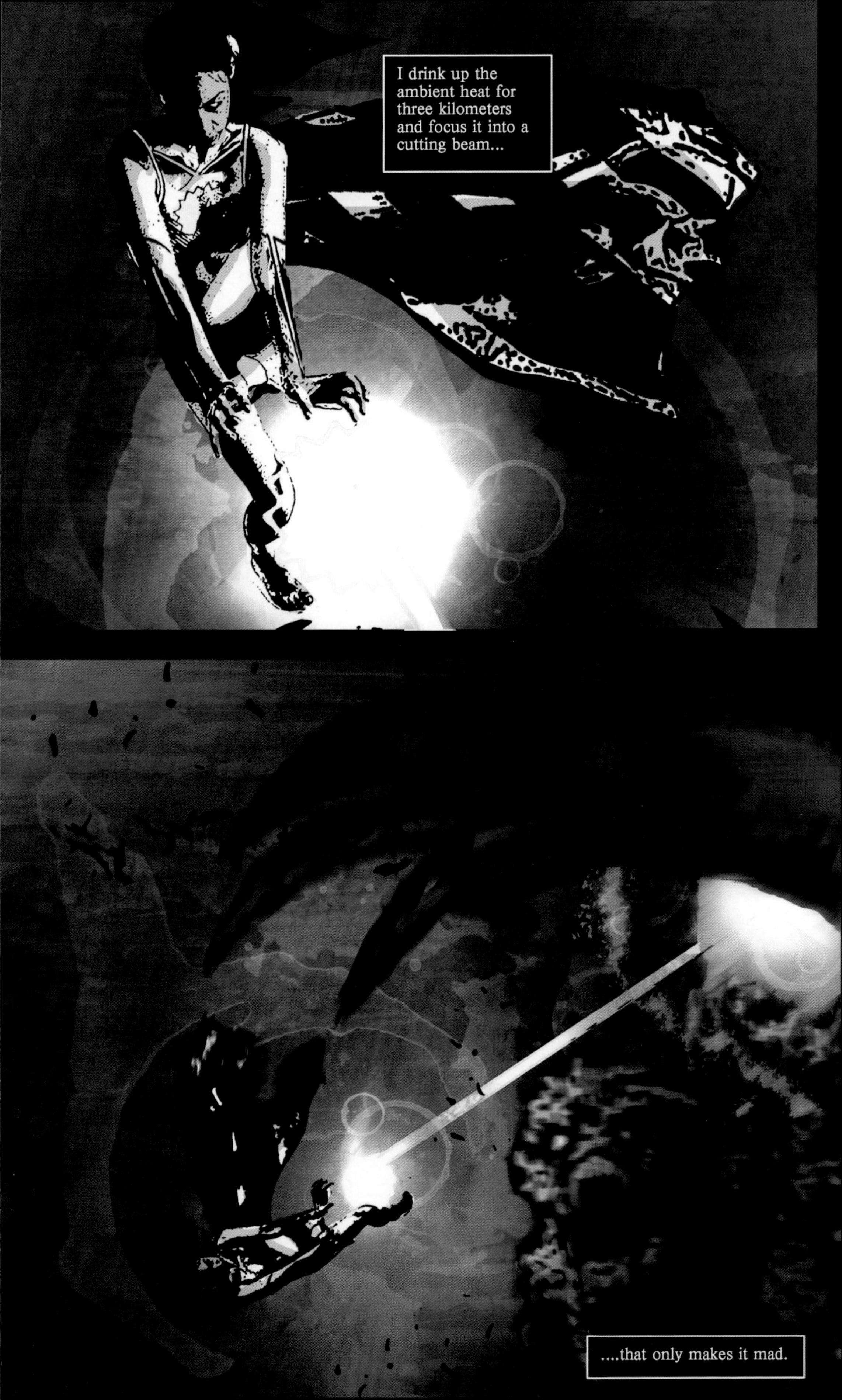
I drink up the ambient heat for three kilometers and focus it into a cutting beam...
....that only makes it mad.

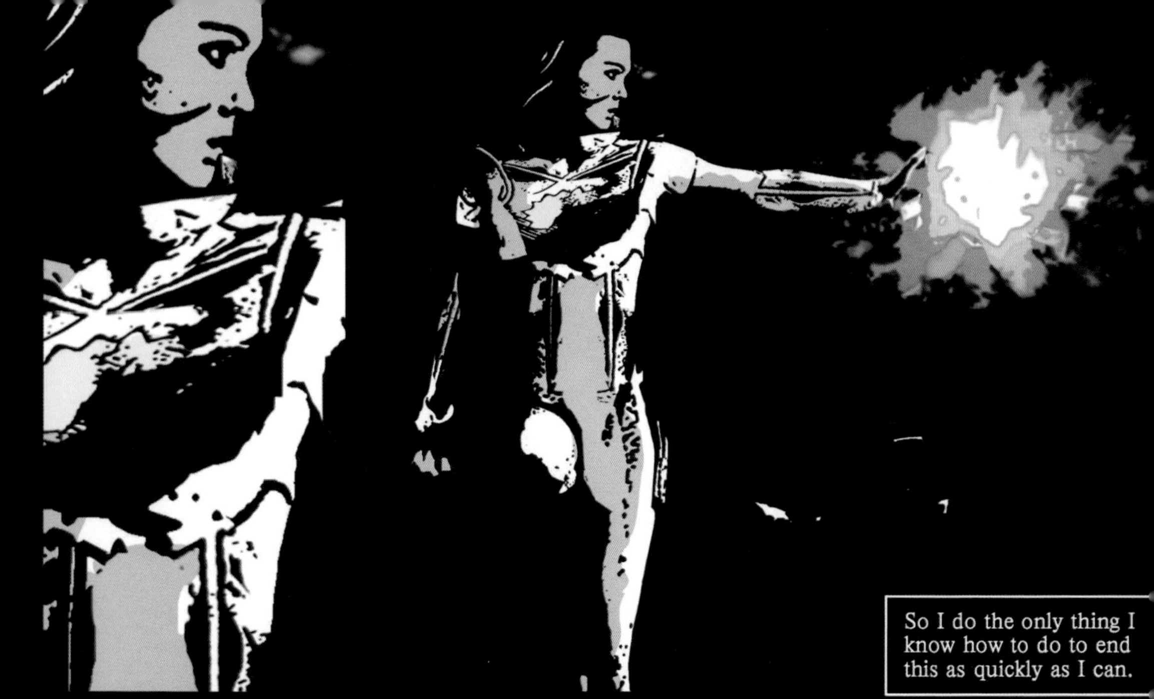
So I do the only thing I know how to do to end this as quickly as I can.

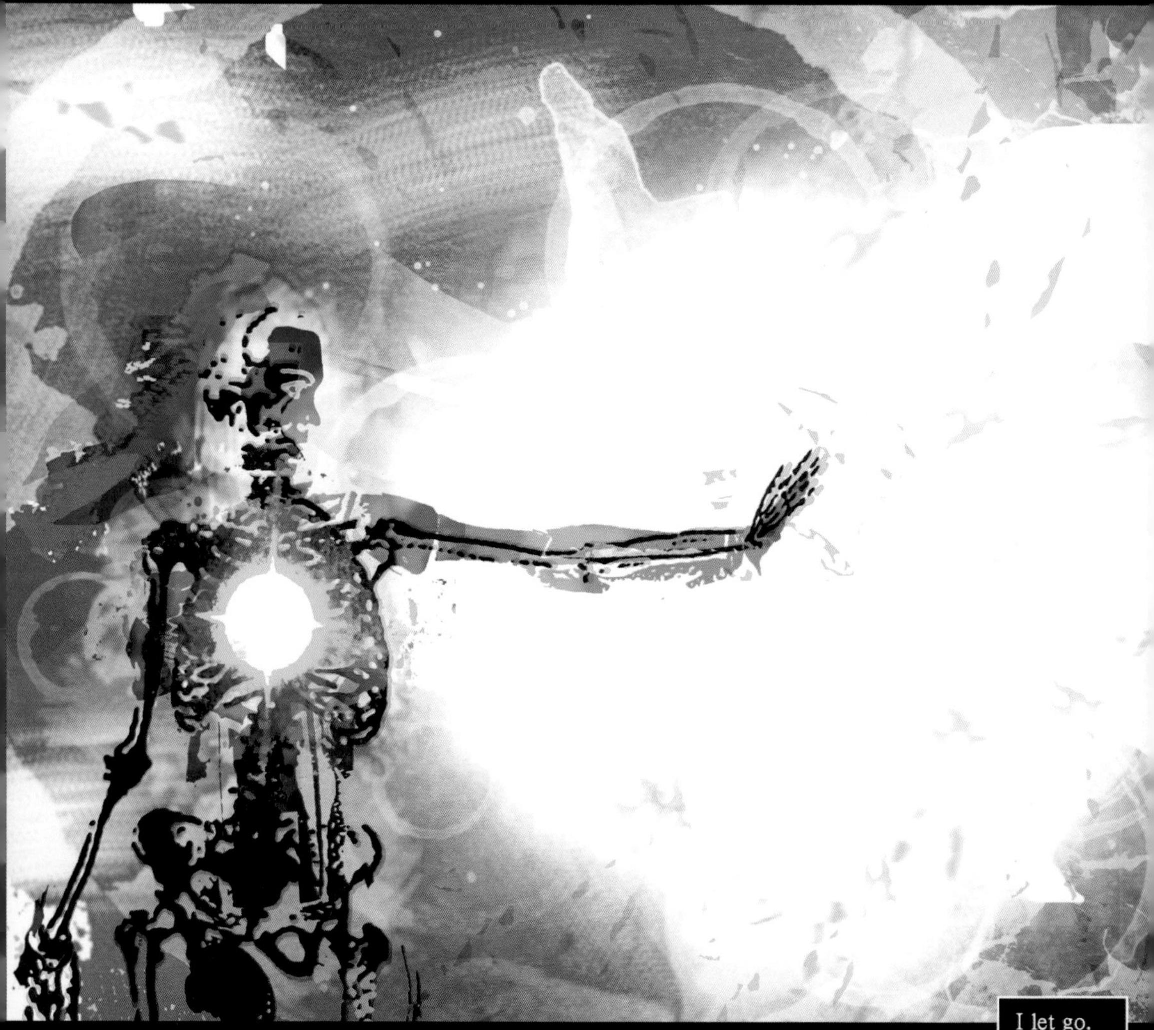
I let go.

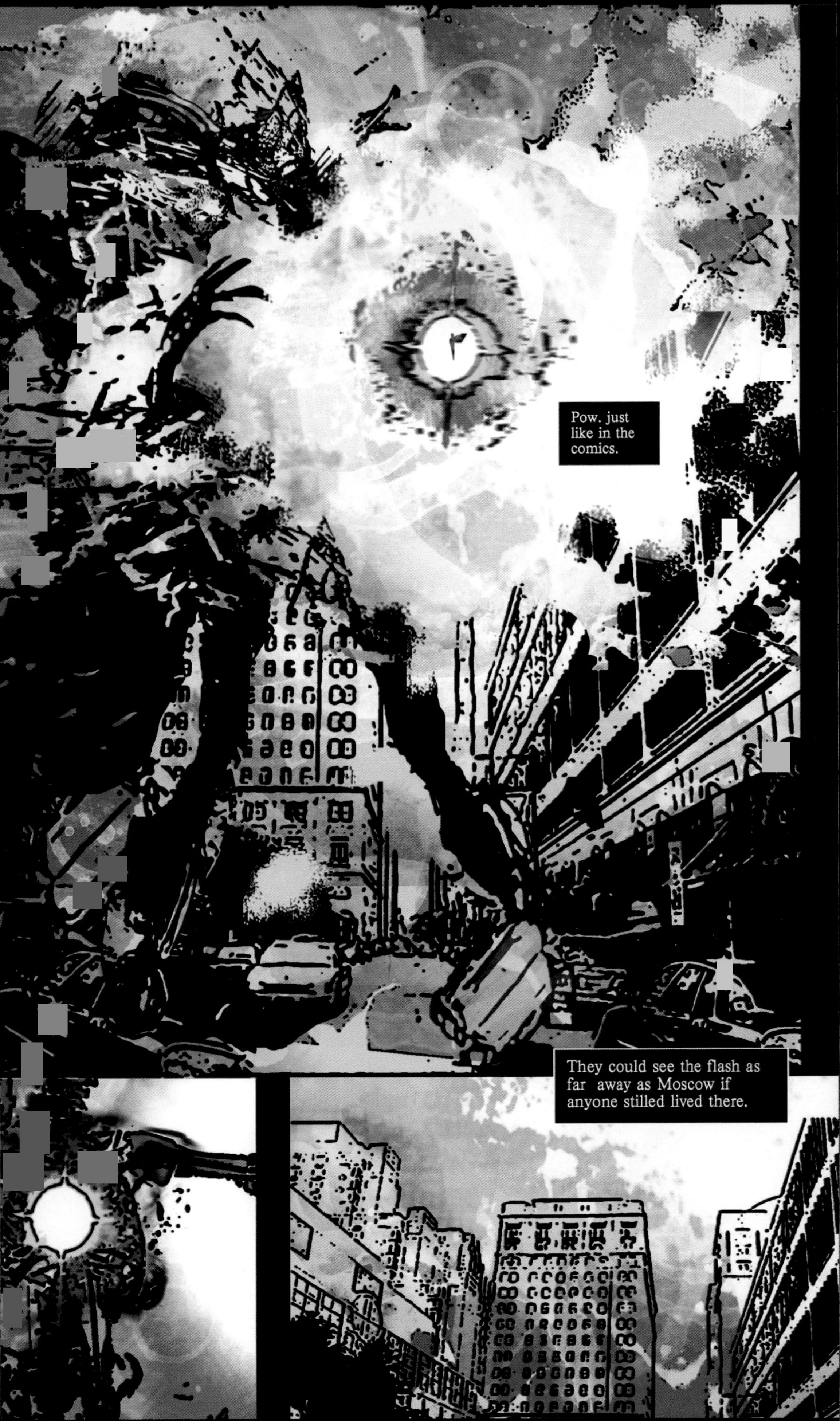
Pow. just like in the comics.
They could see the flash as far away as Moscow if anyone stilled lived there.

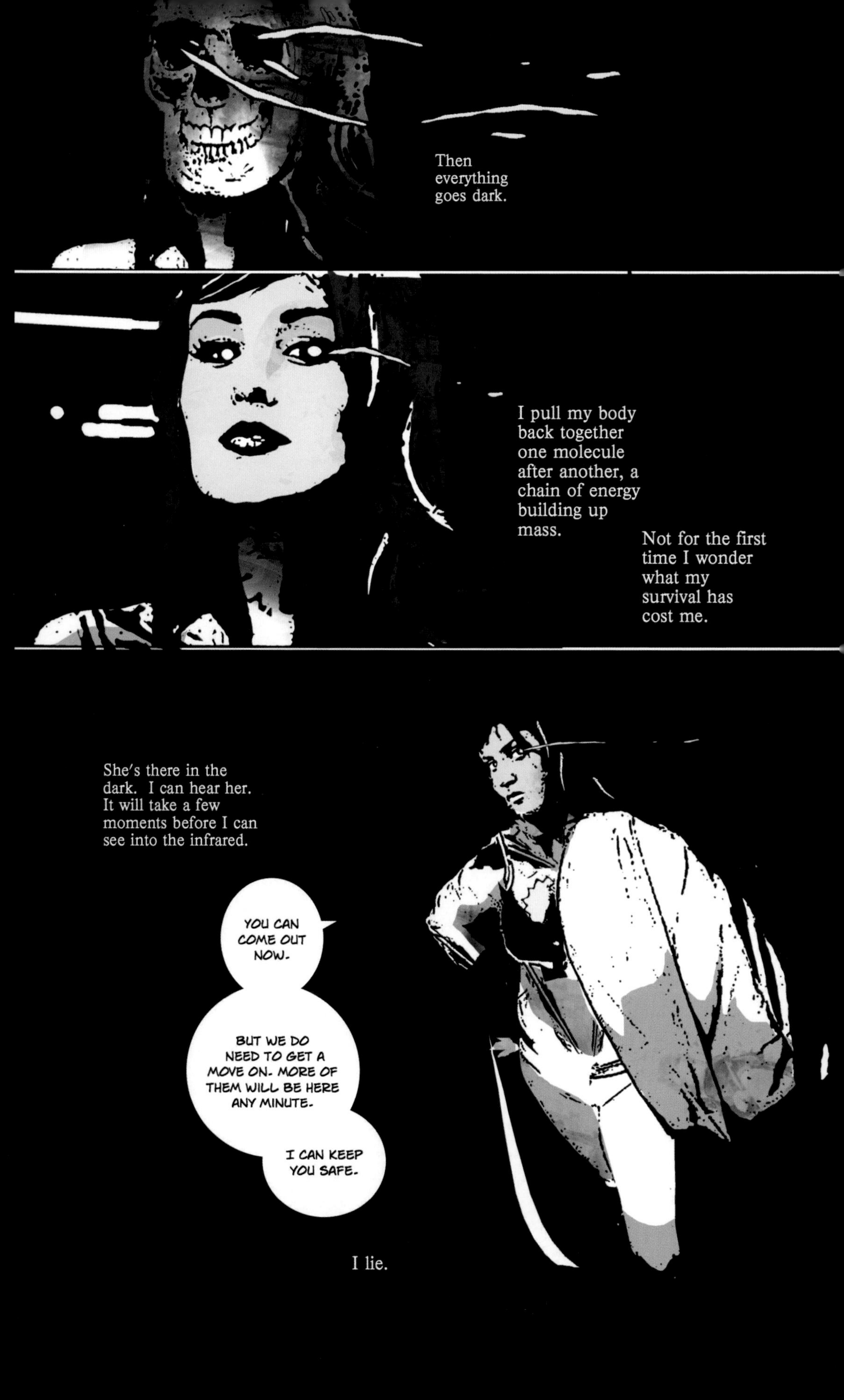
Then everything goes dark.
I pull my body back together one molecule after another, a chain of energy building up mass.
Not for the first time I wonder what my survival has cost me.
She's there in the dark. I can hear her. It will take a few moments before I can see into the infrared.
YOU CAN COME OUT NOW.
BUT WE DO NEED TO GET A MOVE ON. MORE OF THEM WILL BE HERE ANY MINUTE.
I CAN KEEP YOU SAFE.
I lie.

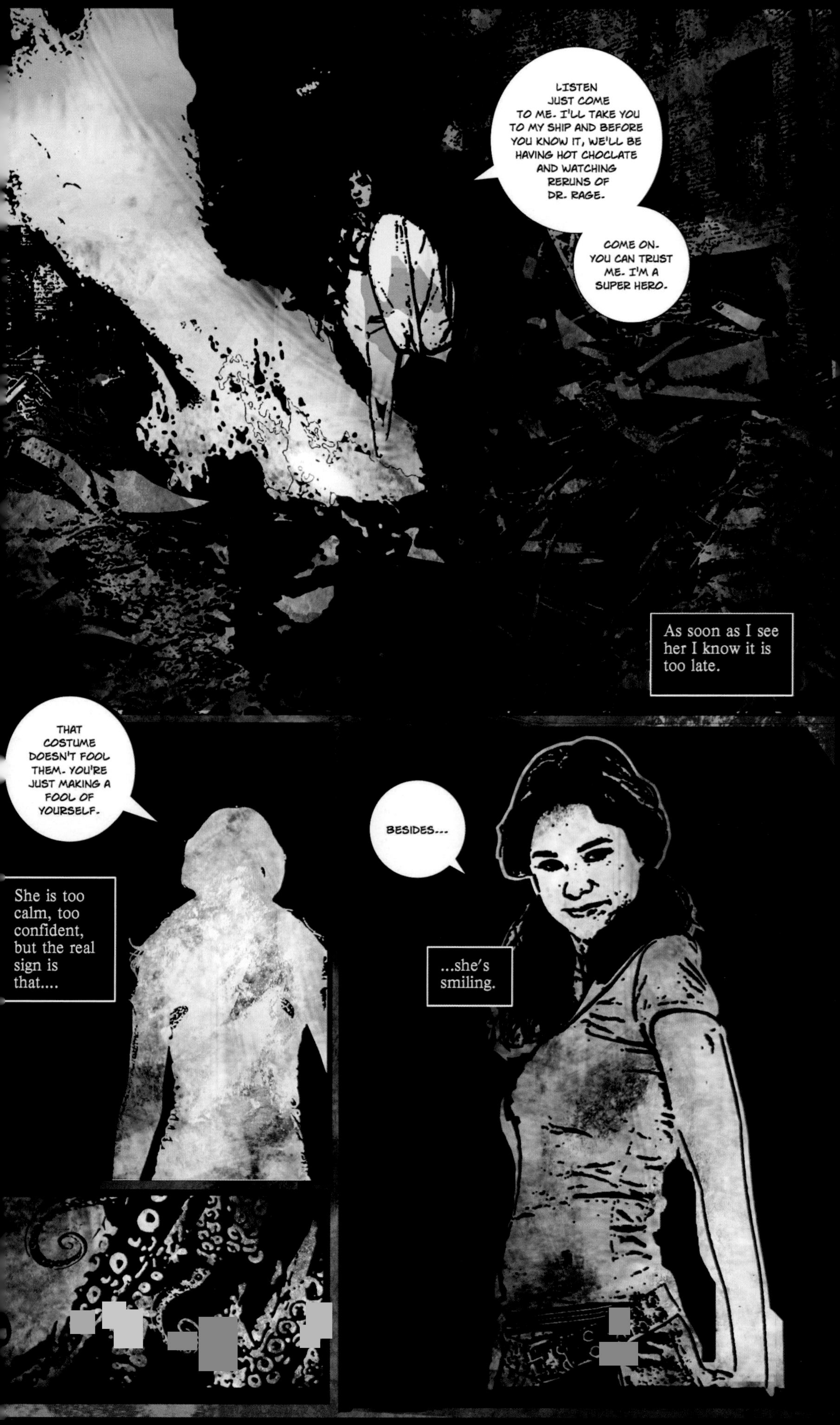
LISTEN JUST COME TO ME. I'LL TAKE YOU TO MY SHIP AND BEFORE YOU KNOW IT, WE'LL BE HAVING HOT CHOCLATE AND WATCHING RERUNS OF DR. RAGE.
COME ON. YOU CAN TRUST ME. I'M A SUPER HERO.
As soon as I see her I know it is too late.
THAT COSTUME DOESN'T FOOL THEM. YOU'RE JUST MAKING A FOOL OF YOURSELF.
She is too calm, too confident, but the real sign is that....
BESIDES...
...she's smiling.

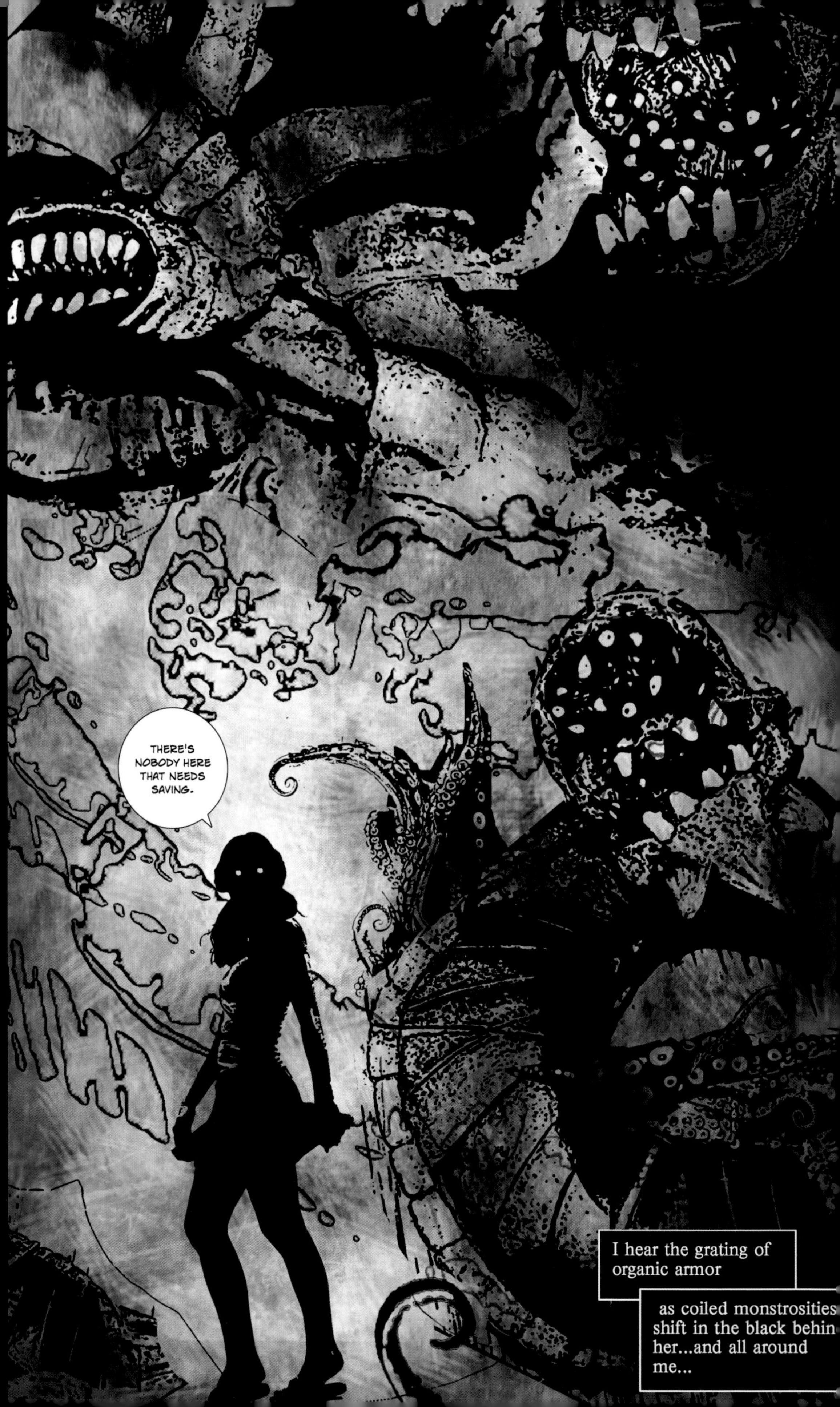
THERE'S NOBODY HERE THAT NEEDS SAVING.
I hear the grating of organic armor
as coiled monstrosities shift in the black behin her...and all around me...

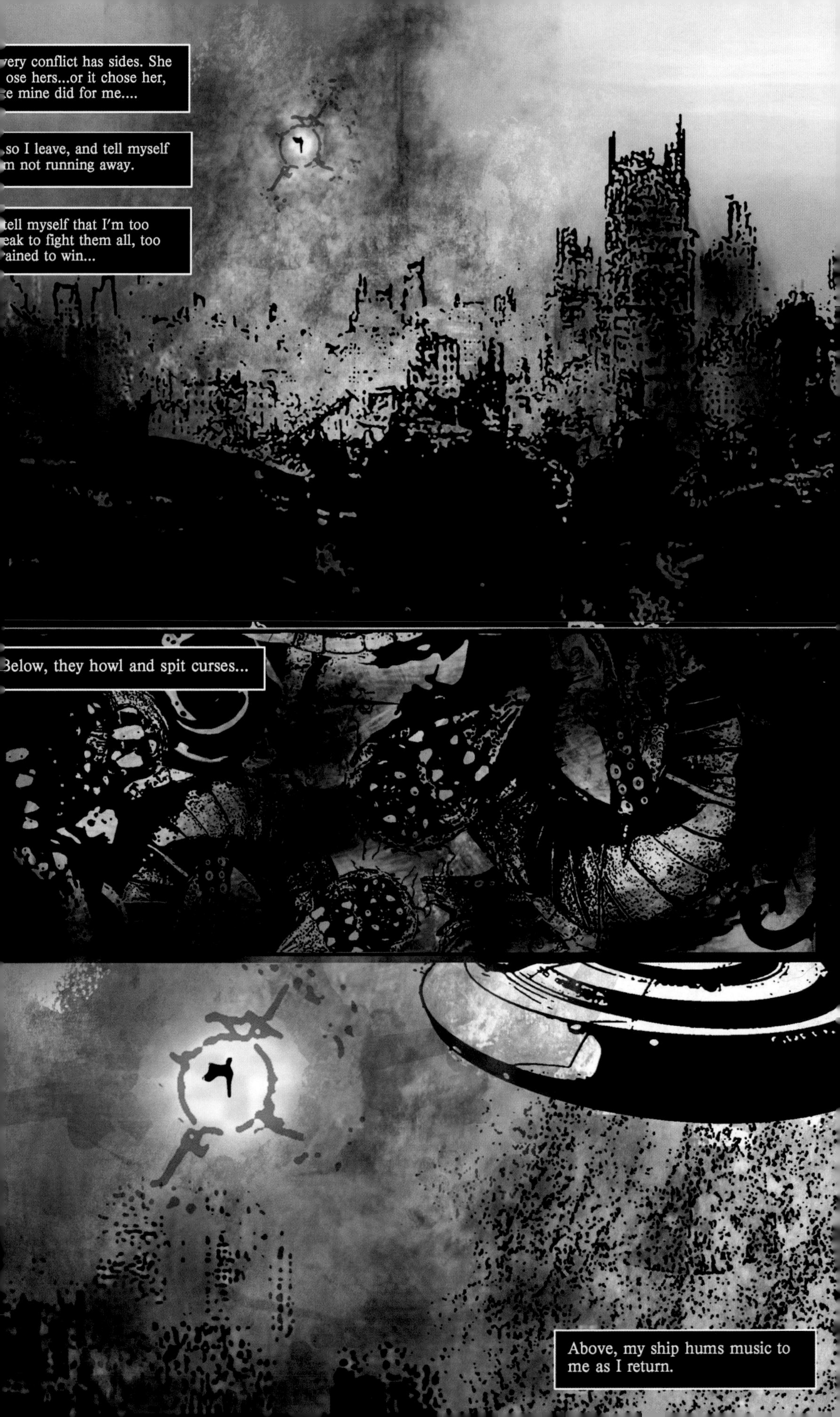
very conflict has sides. She ose hers...or it chose her, e mine did for me....
so I leave, and tell myself m not running away.
tell myself that I'm too eak to fight them all, too ained to win...
Below, they howl and spit curses...
Above, my ship hums music to me as I return.

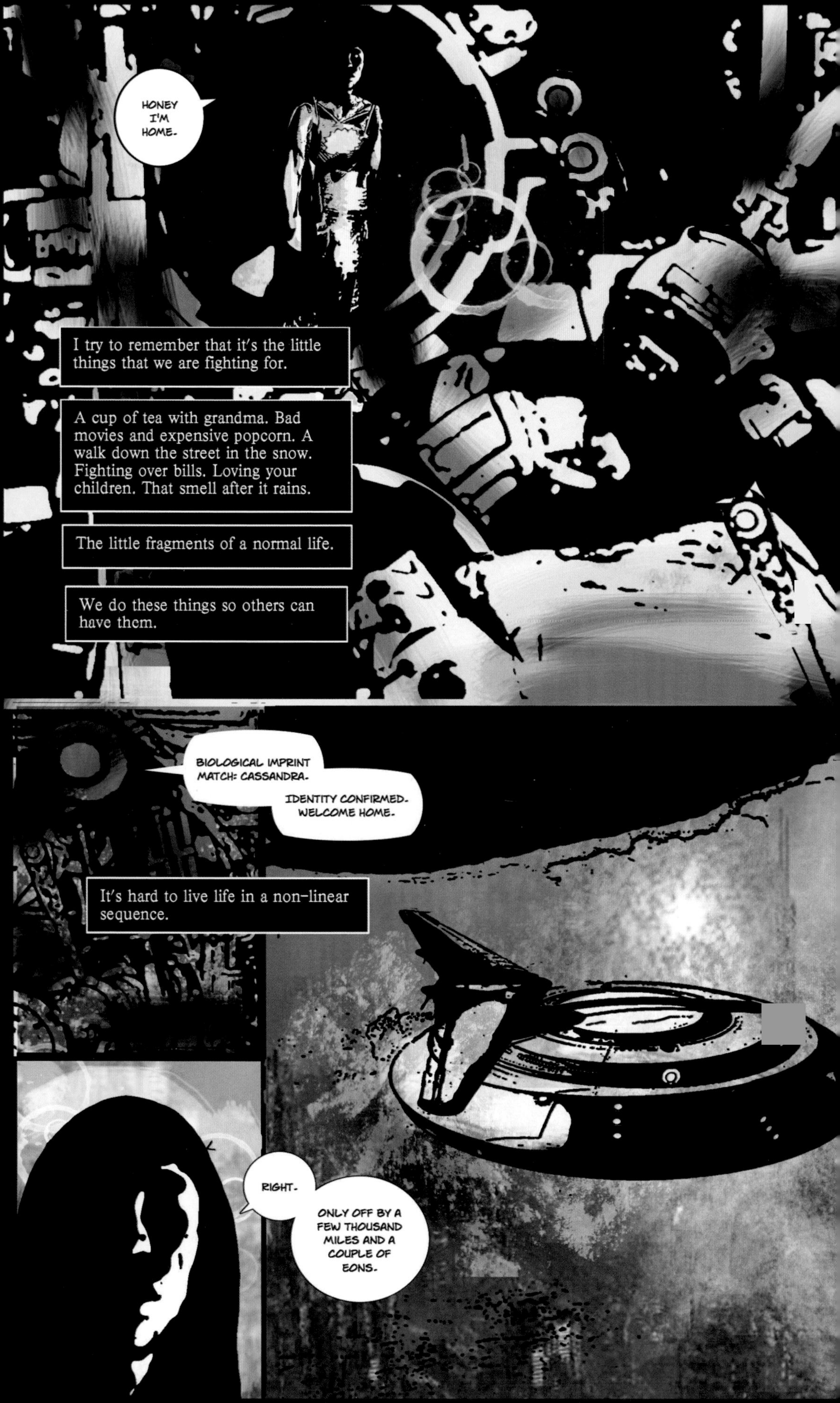
HONEY I'M HOME.
I try to remember that it's the little things that we are fighting for.
A cup of tea with grandma. Bad movies and expensive popcorn. A walk down the street in the snow. Fighting over bills. Loving your children. That smell after it rains.
The little fragments of a normal life.
We do these things so others can have them.
BIOLOGICAL IMPRINT MATCH: CASSANDRA.
IDENTITY CONFIRMED. WELCOME HOME.
It's hard to live life in a non-linear sequence.
RIGHT.
ONLY OFF BY A FEW THOUSAND MILES AND A COUPLE OF EONS.

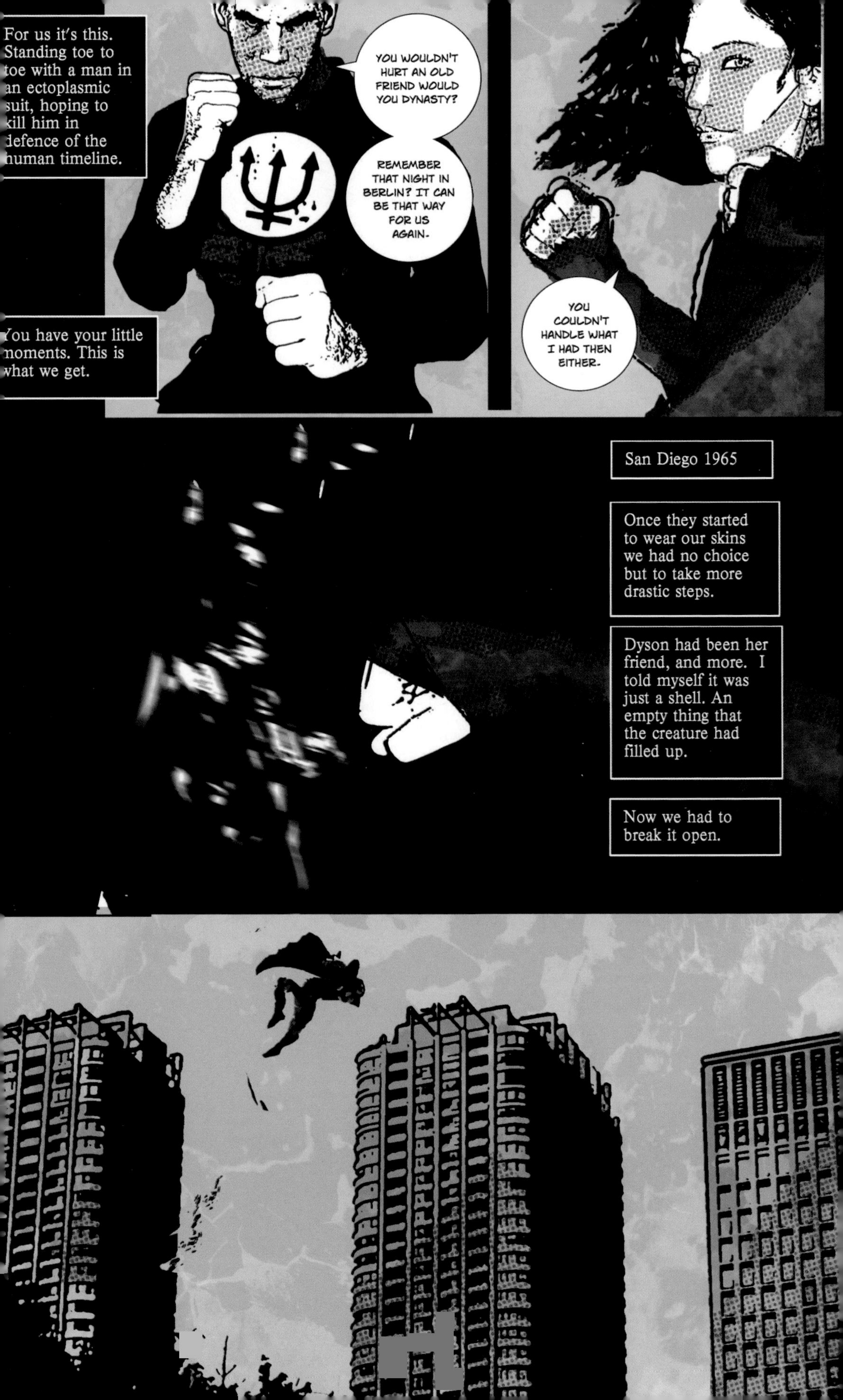

For us it's this. Standing toe to toe with a man in an ectoplasmic suit, hoping to kill him in defence of the human timeline.
YOU WOULDN'T HURT AN OLD FRIEND WOULD YOU DYNASTY?
REMEMBER THAT NIGHT IN BERLIN? IT CAN BE THAT WAY FOR US AGAIN.
You have your little moments. This is what we get.
YOU COULDN'T HANDLE WHAT I HAD THEN EITHER.
San Diego 1965
Once they started to wear our skins we had no choice but to take more drastic steps.
Dyson had been her friend, and more. I told myself it was just a shell. An empty thing that the creature had filled up.
Now we had to break it open.

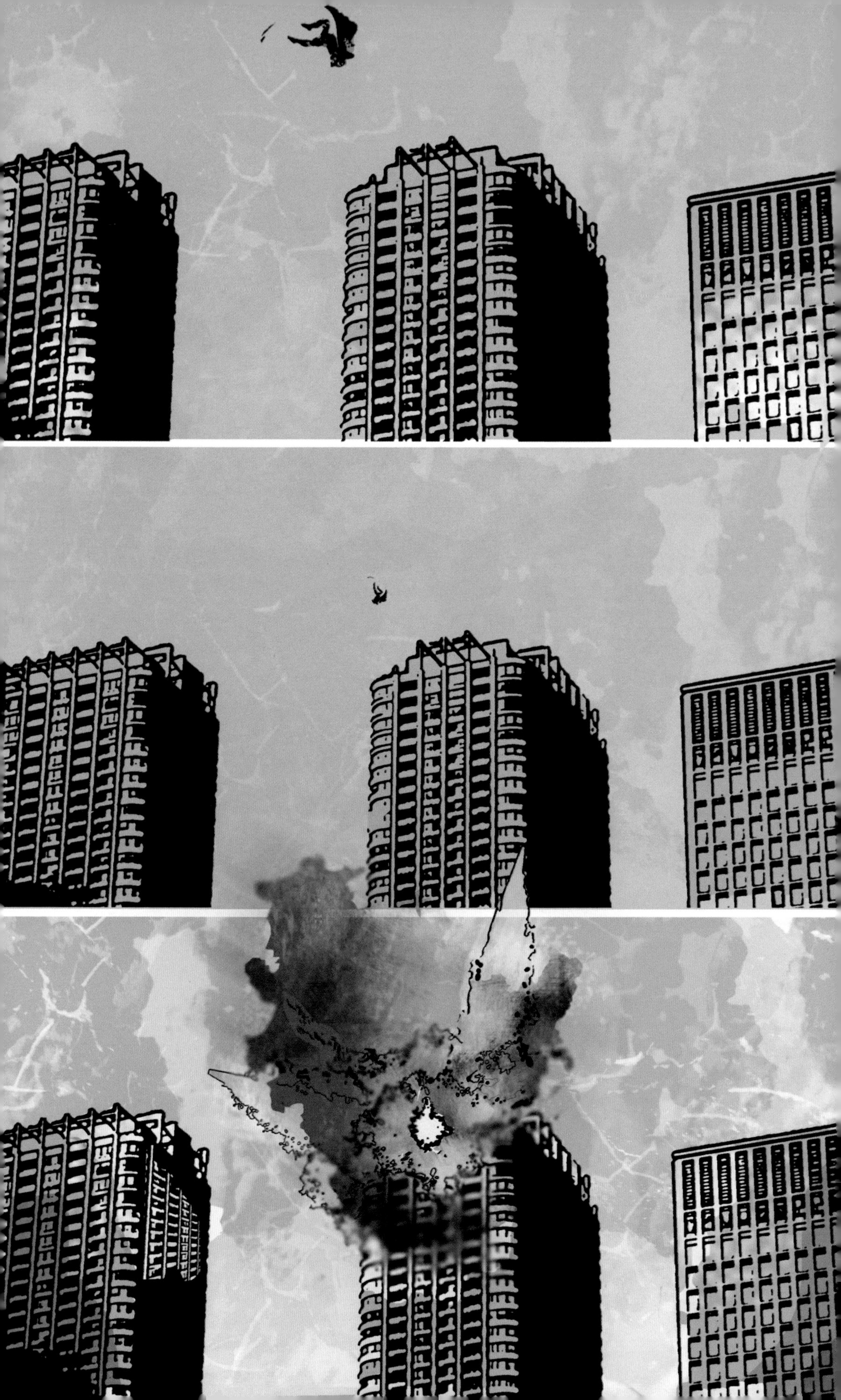

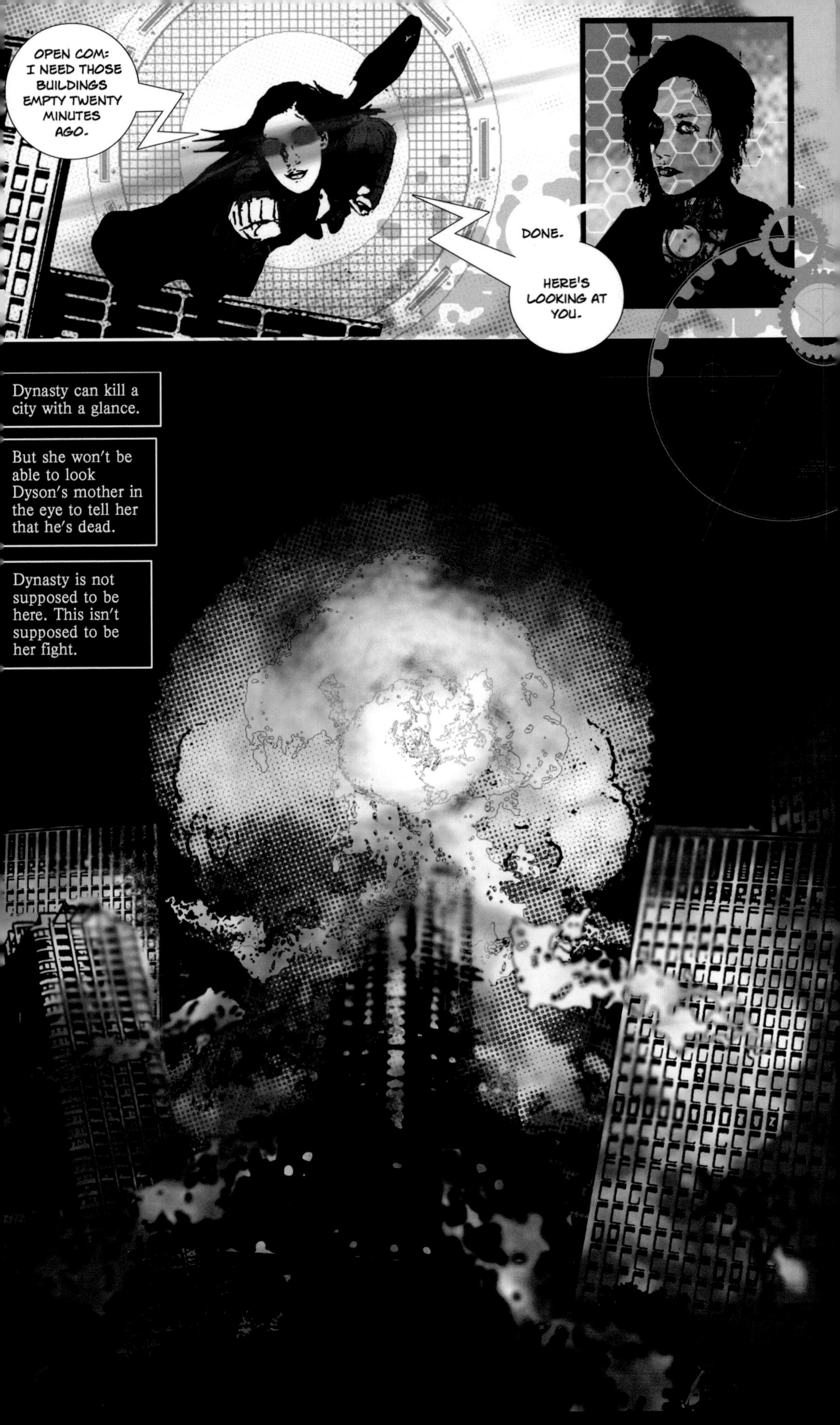
OPEN COM: I NEED THOSE BUILDINGS EMPTY TWENTY MINUTES AGO.
DONE.
HERE'S LOOKING AT YOU.
Dynasty can kill a city with a glance.
But she won't be able to look Dyson's mother in the eye to tell her that he's dead.
Dynasty is not supposed to be here. This isn't supposed to be her fight.

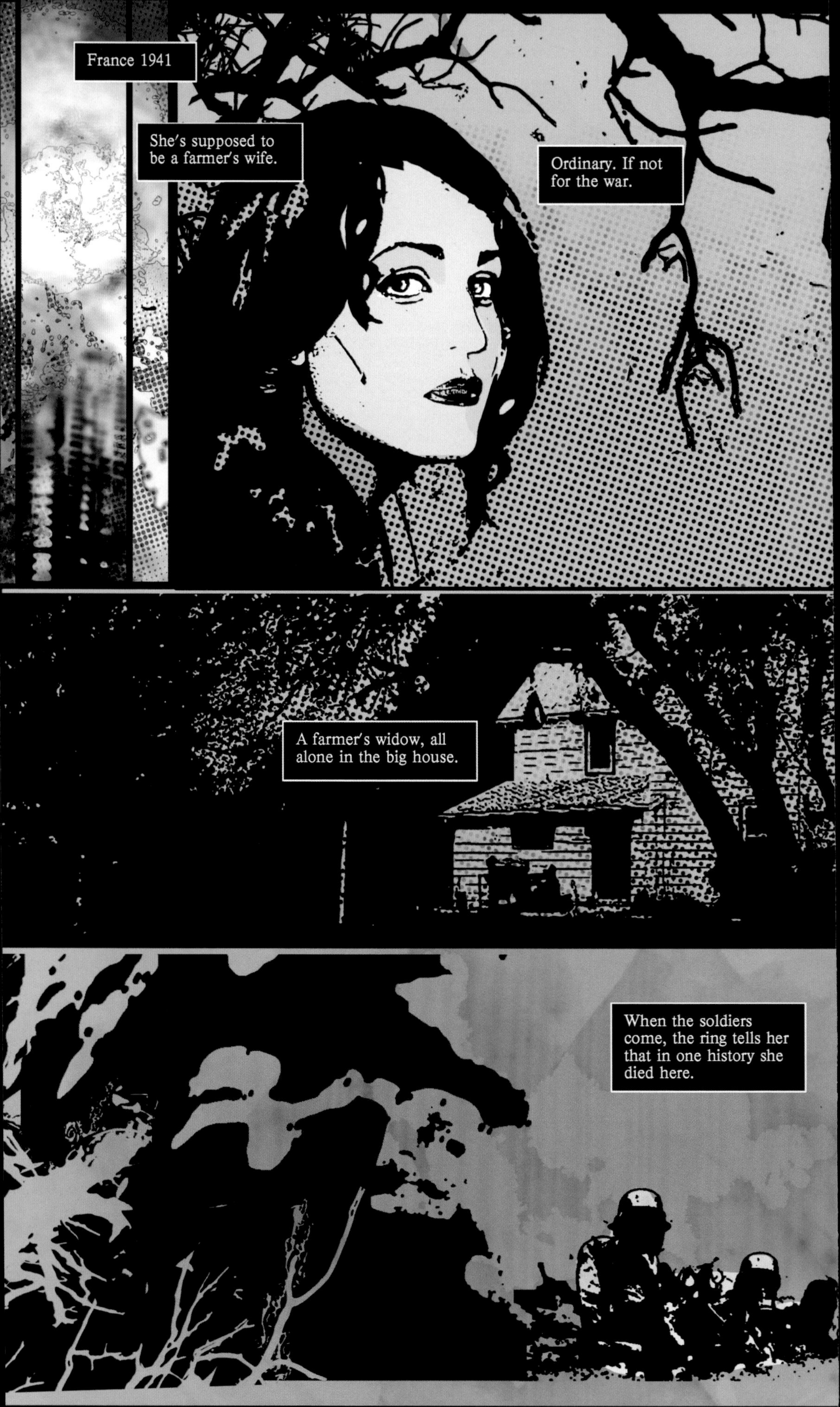
France 1941
She's supposed to be a farmer's wife.
Ordinary. If not for the war.
A farmer's widow, all alone in the big house.
When the soldiers come, the ring tells her that in one history she died here.

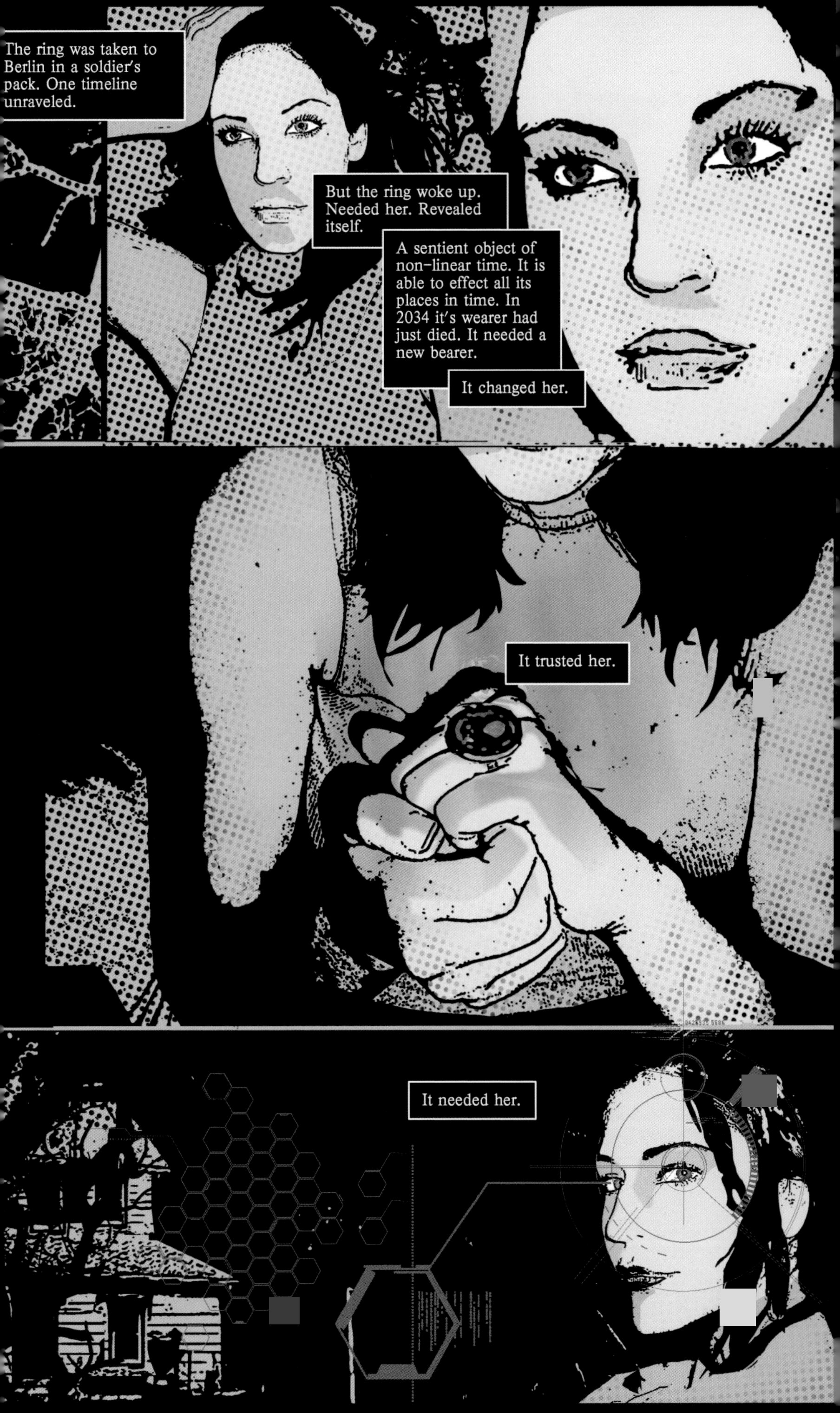
The ring was taken to Berlin in a soldier's pack. One timeline unraveled.
But the ring woke up. Needed her. Revealed itself.
A sentient object of non-linear time. It is able to effect all its places in time. In 2034 it's wearer had just died. It needed a new bearer.
It changed her.
It trusted her.
It needed her.

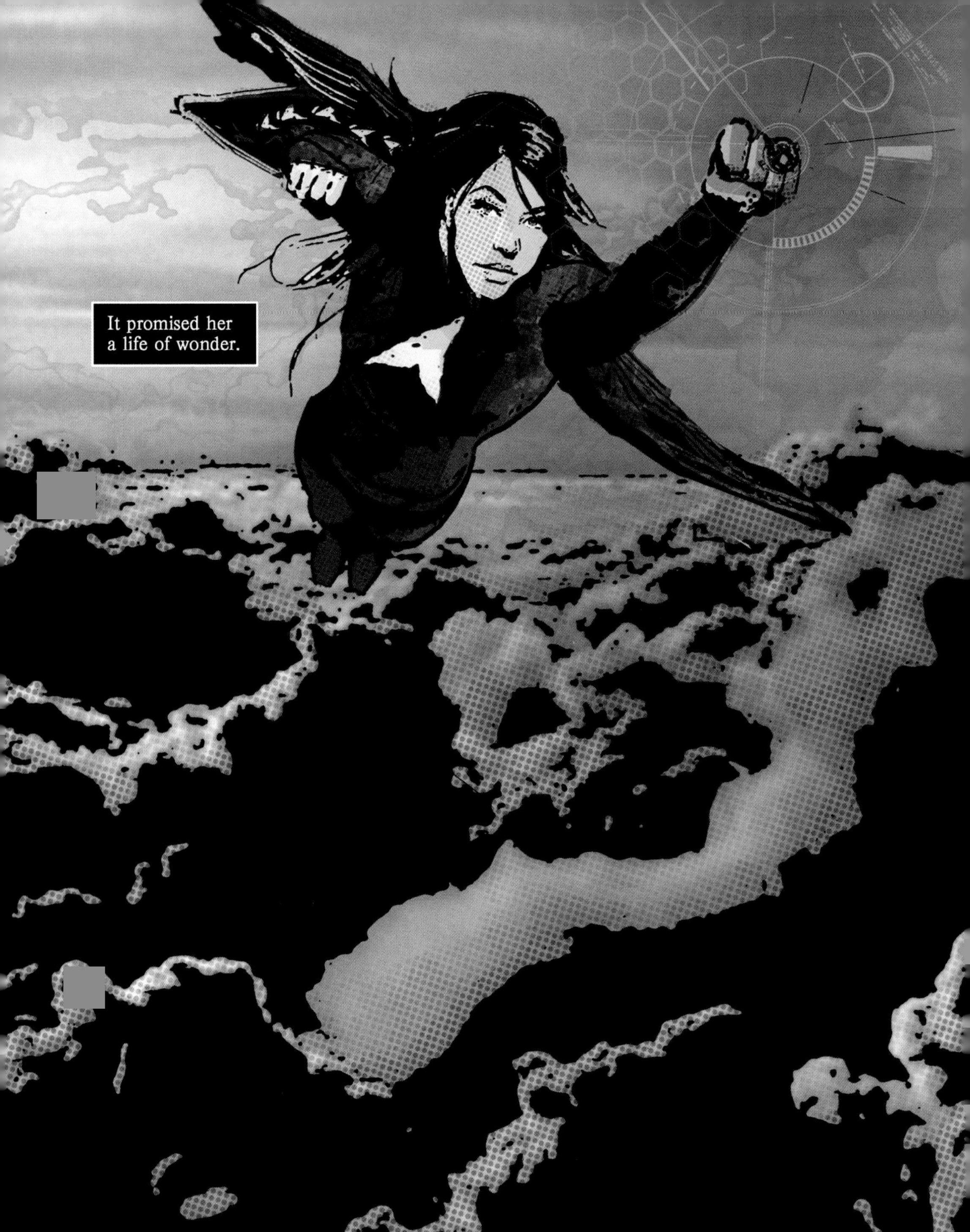
It promised her
a life of wonder.

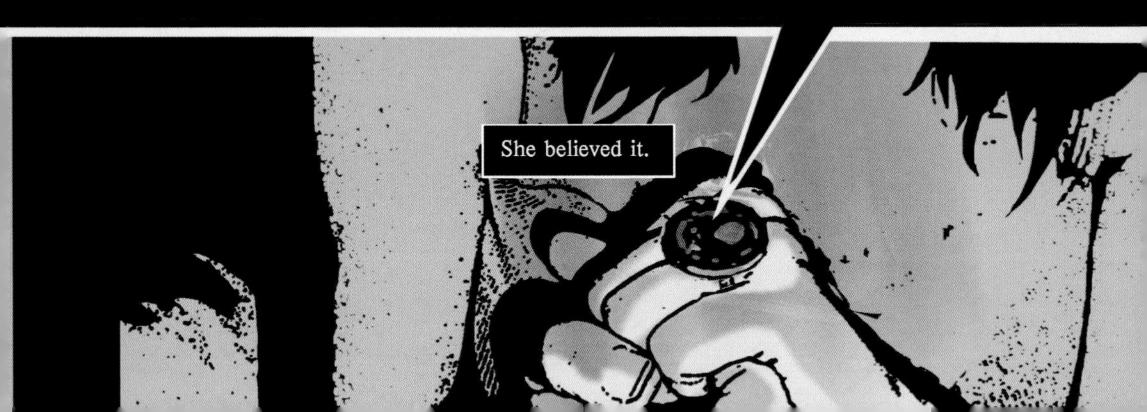
She believed it.

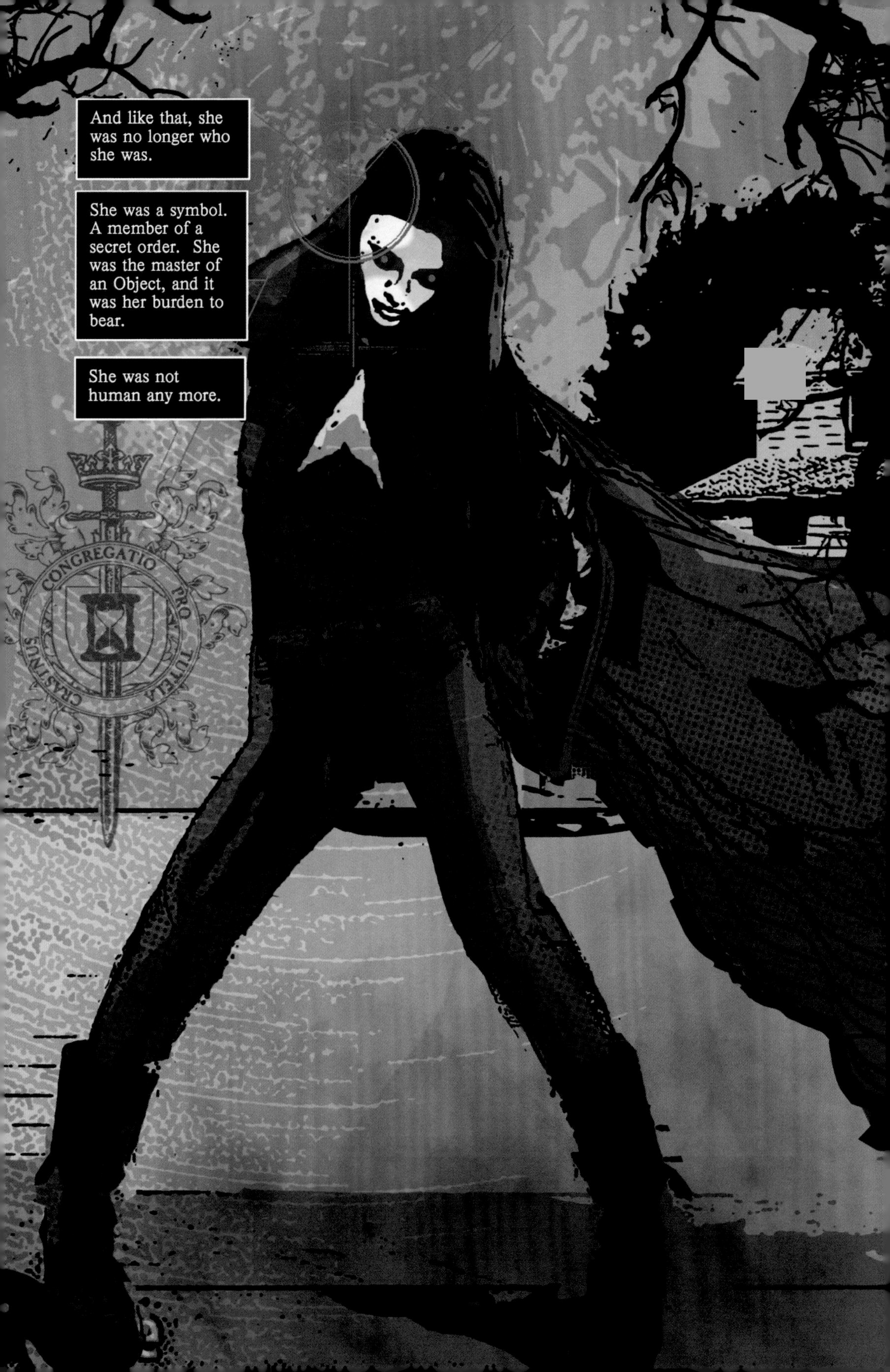
And like that, she was no longer who she was.
She was a symbol. A member of a secret order. She was the master of an Object, and it was her burden to bear.
She was not human any more.
CONGREGATIO PRO TUTELA CRASTINUS

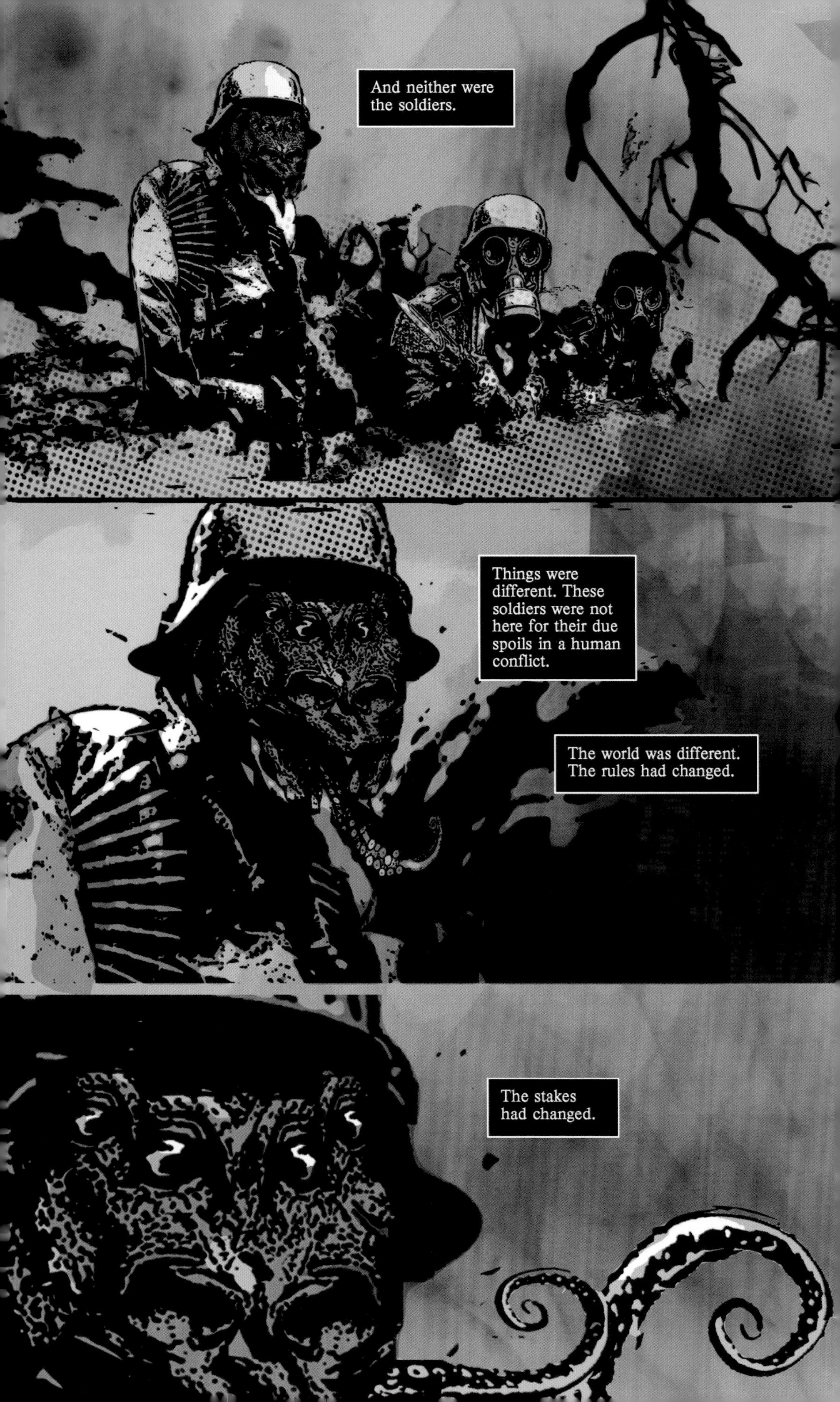
And neither were the soldiers.
Things were different. These soldiers were not here for their due spoils in a human conflict.
The world was different. The rules had changed.
The stakes had changed.

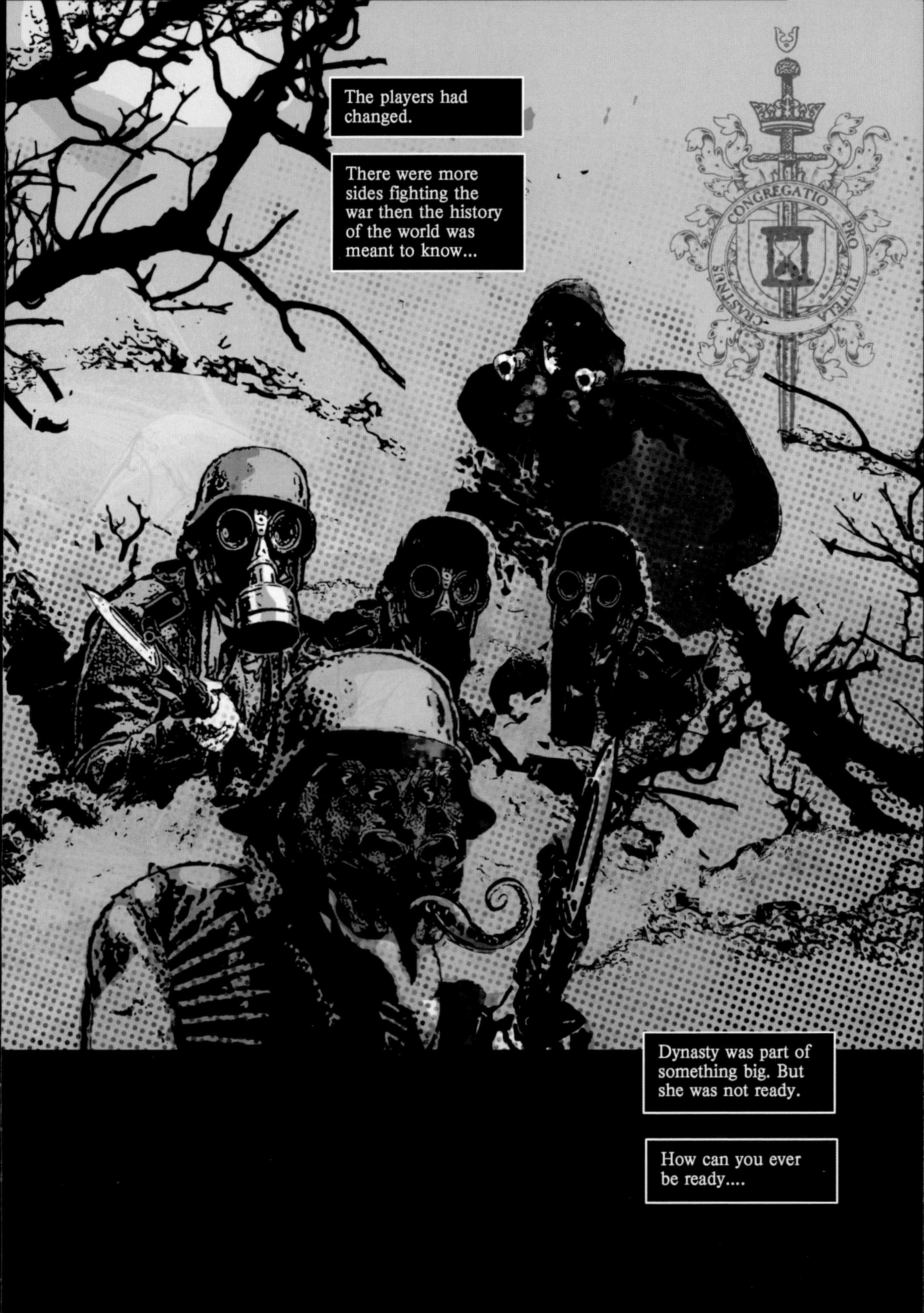
The players had changed.
There were more sides fighting the war then the history of the world was meant to know...
CONGREGATIO PRO TUTELA CRASTINUS
Dynasty was part of something big. But she was not ready.
How can you ever be ready....

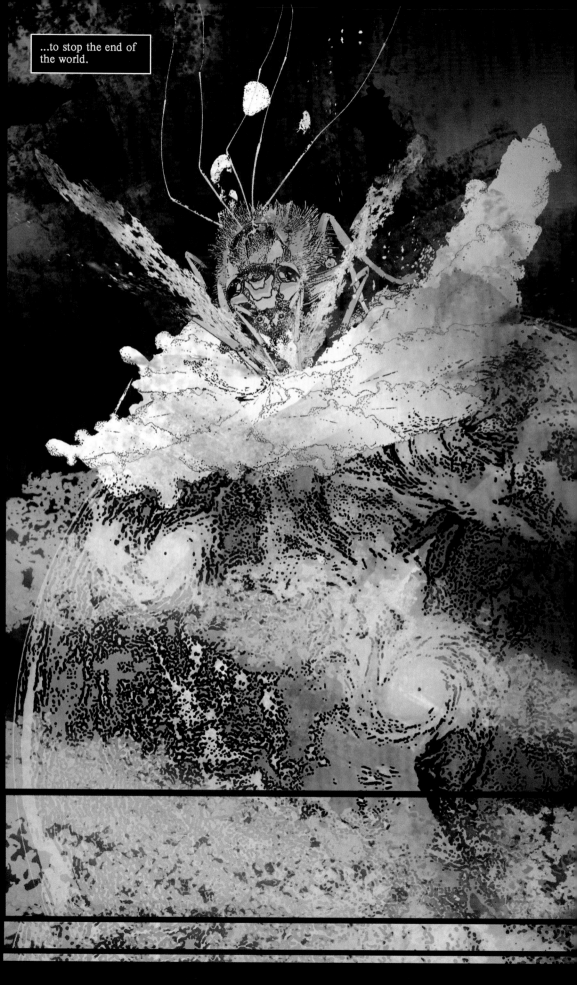

...to stop the end of the world.

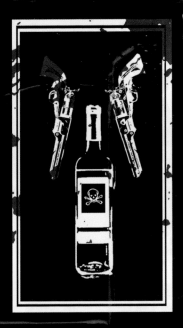

SIXGUN

QUIXOTE ™

dime novel poetry by
john toone
gmb chomichuk

virtual blip
nothing but

crickets and wooden nickels
twisting and turning and

dropping dead
face up
frozen in time
as luck would have it
misplaced
and forgotten

Knowing where home
is, and knowing how
to get there are not
the same thing.

The road is crooked
and filled with
snakes.

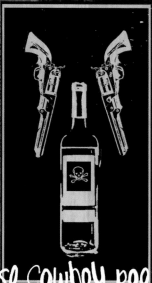

those cowboy poems

claims he
owns the place
he flipped
big hat to fill
with change
excuses and lies
he reckons he is
righting

Road agents want his horse. Three o[redacted]hem. They are talking, laughing[redacted]surrounding. One moment l[redacted] to make the outcome his.

The iron comes up, polish-bright in the cloudless sunshine. Hammer-snap throws fire smoke and lead. The road agent's jaw flaps away, tumbling in a wet red cloud. He turns, all things hinged[redacted]to his hip, and the gun. The se[redacted]ond shot punches the second[redacted]man hard in the chest. The third man is a lucky shot. Married to surprise, the gunfight's mistress is luck. No time left to aim, no initiative left to pray, he points and squeezes[redacted]one two three four click cl[redacted] click. The smoke hides the body from him. But he knows it is laying there, because he is still standing here.

There are silver dollars in their pockets and a watch on a chain.

He puts the money in his pocket and hangs the watch on the branc[redacted] the tree. He has too much [redacted] already.

$

"You took their money." The gambler flips the cards.

"I make my living with the skills I have. What else can I do?"

"I look at the skills I have and ask 'What else can I do?'"

"Killing and being a killer are not the same."

"Aren't they? The money I have comes from the pockets of men that might have disagreed."

"They aren't here to argue. I only listen to voices. Not ghosts."

"Then I disagree."

"You aren't living, that makes you a ghost. Live a little then I'll listen. Have a seat."

He plays cards with dead men's money. He loses it, but he's made a friend.

$

The gambler is a lunger. When he isn't drinking he is coughing. He wipes his red lips on his pink linen kerchief. He walks with a slow and deliberate measure. Each step is a gift the man decides, and shares his water and jerk with the gambler who took his money.

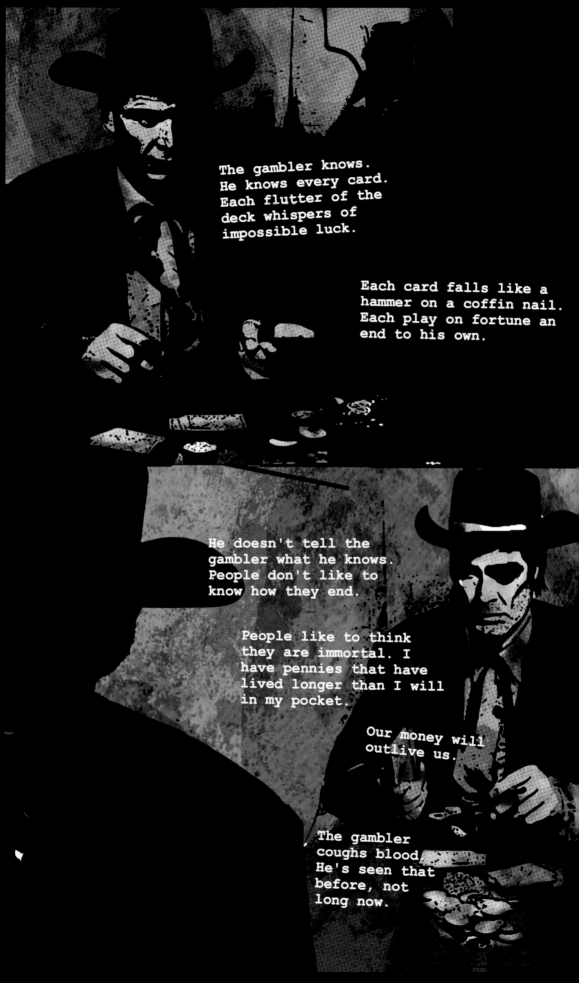

The gambler knows.
He knows every card.
Each flutter of the
deck whispers of
impossible luck.

Each card falls like a
hammer on a coffin nail.
Each play on fortune an
end to his own.

He doesn't tell the
gambler what he knows.
People don't like to
know how they end.

People like to think
they are immortal. I
have pennies that have
lived longer than I will
in my pocket.

Our money will
outlive us.

The gambler
coughs blood.
He's seen that
before, not
long now.

under the bridge on postcards
giant fighting shadows blur
and it is blowing like the dickens
over the clicking machinery at sals
pigeons picking away
at boot leather and soles
moths against the florescence
clapping as the clouds open/close

"There is a way out...
but the road does not lead
where you think it
does..."the gambler says...

On the way to the next watering
they laugh and curse and spit.
He sees that the gambler does
not have long.

$

He wakes up to crows. They are
all over him. On his companion.
The gambler is dead. The man
strips him naked, the clothes
for him, the skin for the birds.
$

The watering hole is a shiny
dime on the dark and distant
ground.

The horse drinks and drinks from
moonlit water.

He fills his belly, then his
skins. There is an overturned
wagon, blackened with fire.
Under it is a quarter-full tin
of flour and knife that still
has an edge. Under the wagon is
the skull of a boy.

feeding the nettles and thistles
spilling over the shell casings
of creatures that are slow to vacuum
the contours of river bottom

fingers behind ears coaxing
stirring not slowing
drawing him to the underbelly
magnifications of the future

$

The road is a thin suggestion
beneath the dust. He wonders if
he imagines it; this road home.

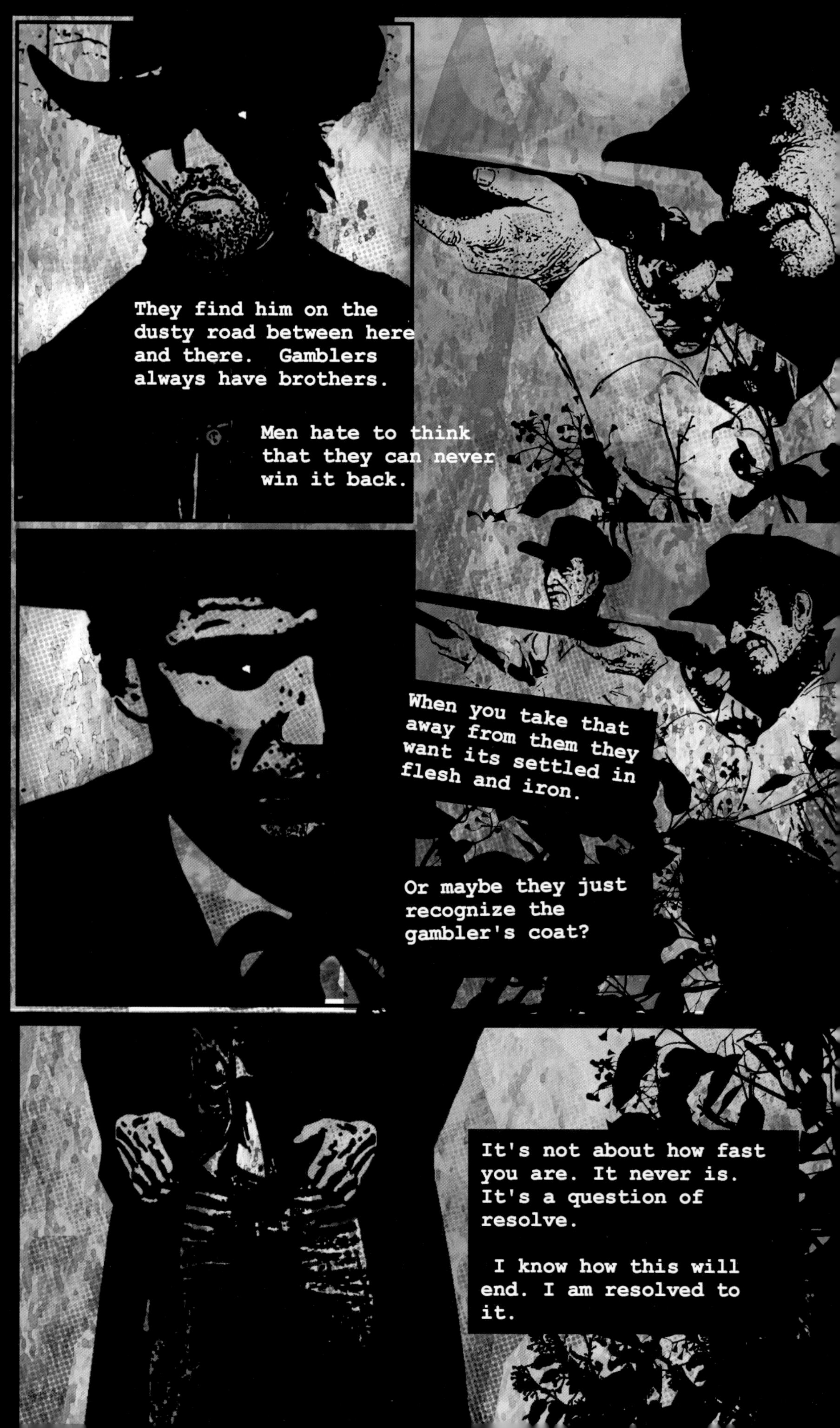
They find him on the dusty road between here and there. Gamblers always have brothers.
Men hate to think that they can never win it back.
When you take that away from them they want its settled in flesh and iron.
Or maybe they just recognize the gambler's coat?
It's not about how fast you are. It never is. It's a question of resolve.
I know how this will end. I am resolved to it.

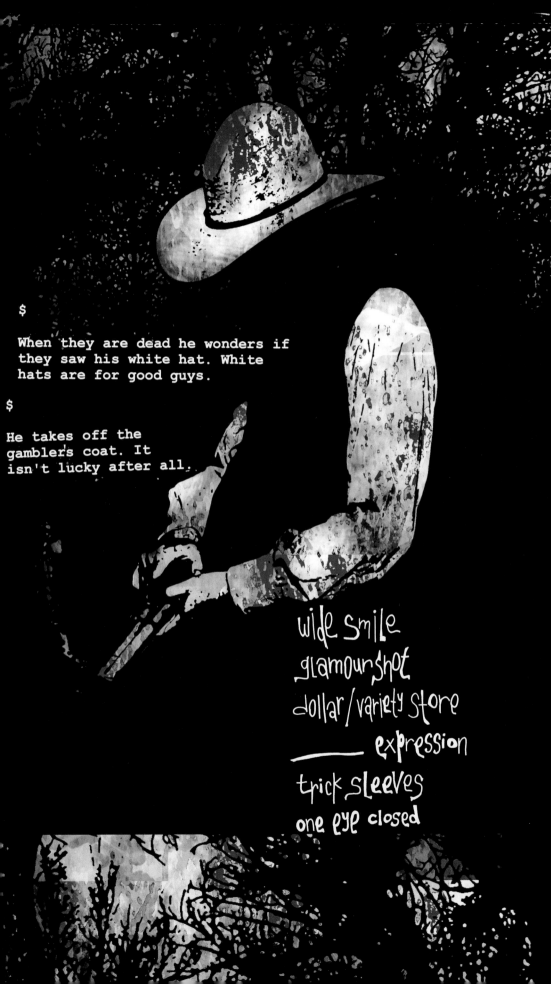

$

When they are dead he wonders if
they saw his white hat. White
hats are for good guys.

$

He takes off the
gambler's coat. It
isn't lucky after all.

wide smile
glamourshot
dollar/variety store
_____ expression
trick sleeves
one eye closed

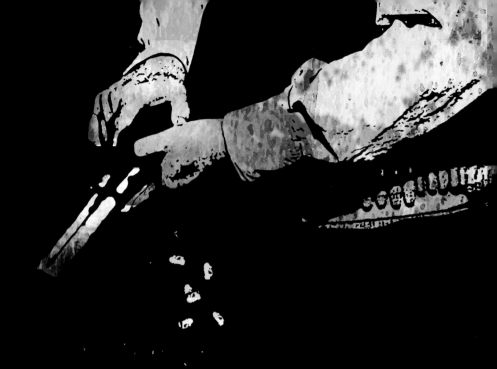

Six empty shells
clatter on the
ground. Used and
useless.

$

He's sure he had to. He's sure
he's a good guy.

bottled up
message lights
lost then found
sent home
after the fact
repatriated

$

The road is long and dry.
He needs a drink.

$

Up ahead is a tree. Maybe
he'll find shelter. Shade.

$

There is a man in the tree.
Strung up and withered.
This stranger has hung
himself. The wind puts its
fingers in his pockets and
pulls things out to look
at. Bits of paper flutter
in the gravel at his feet.

One of the pieces lifts up,
twisting in the wind like
an insect. It sticks the
horses lathered hide,
turning from pale to dark
as the sweat soaks in the
paper.

$

two sheets to the wind
dead end to dead end
wearing thin the main strip
boulevard swaggering
dressed to kill, grin
"no fuckin' mercy" screaming

$
At first the gun seemed
a luxury. But it is a
dead weight that anchors
him to a past. Too short
ranged to bring food,
too heavy to carry and
not be water. But now
that he has seen the
swinging body in the
tree, the gun has
another purpose. Now the
gun is a way to leave
the road if he has too.
He carries it now as a
way to make sure that
the sun cannot have him.

of two cents stretched
a few belts too many
the crushing grip and brow wipe
is full steam clear ahead
his heel toe shuffle captured by
camera phones chattering away

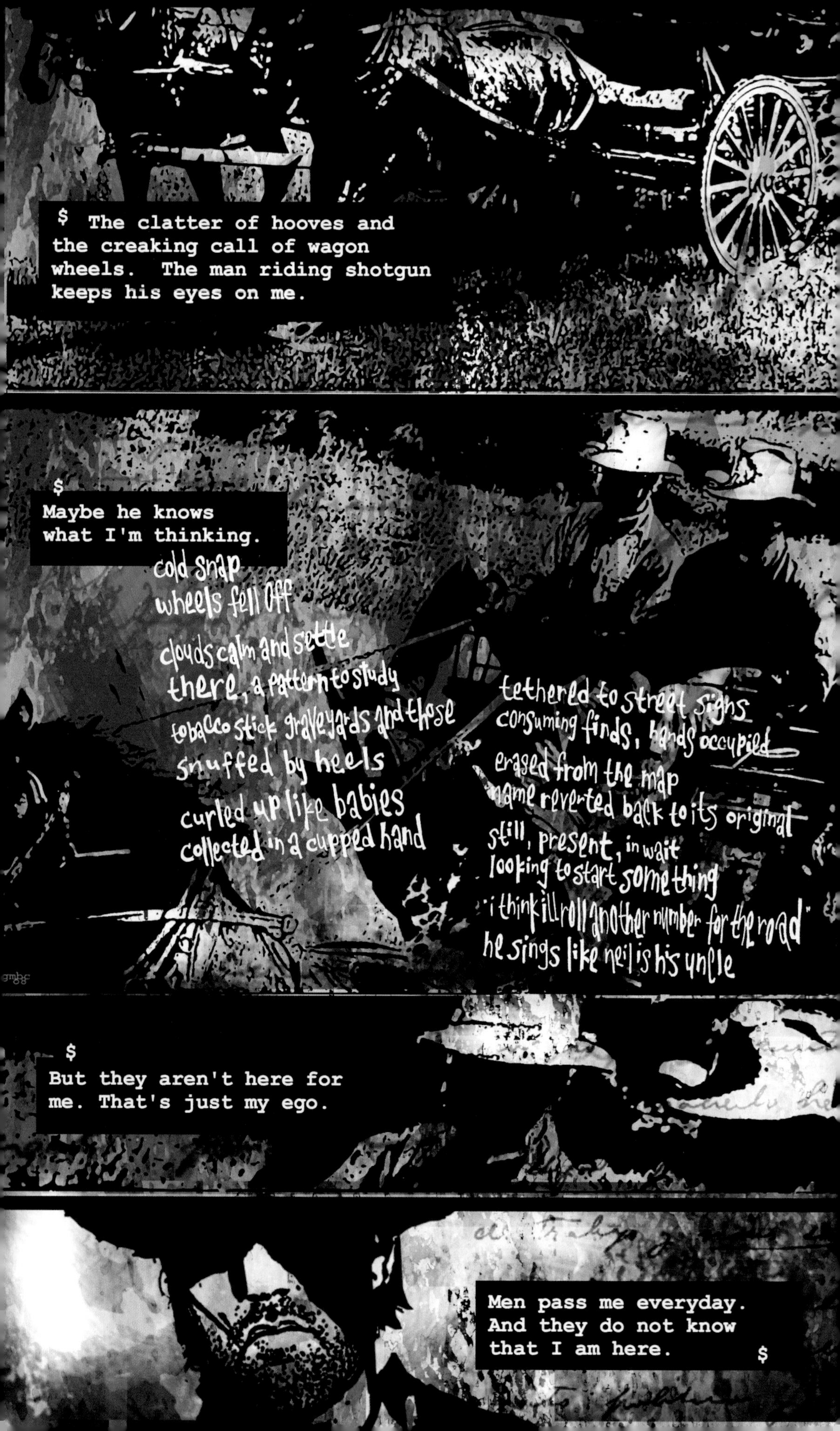

$ The clatter of hooves and the creaking call of wagon wheels. The man riding shotgun keeps his eyes on me.

$ Maybe he knows what I'm thinking.

cold snap
wheels fell off

clouds calm and settle
there, a pattern to study
tobacco stick graveyards and those
snuffed by heels
curled up like babies
collected in a cupped hand

tethered to street signs
consuming finds, hands occupied
erased from the map
name reverted back to its original
still, present, in wait
looking to start something
i think ill roll another number for the road
he sings like neil is his uncle

$ But they aren't here for me. That's just my ego.

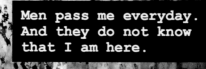

Men pass me everyday. And they do not know that I am here. $

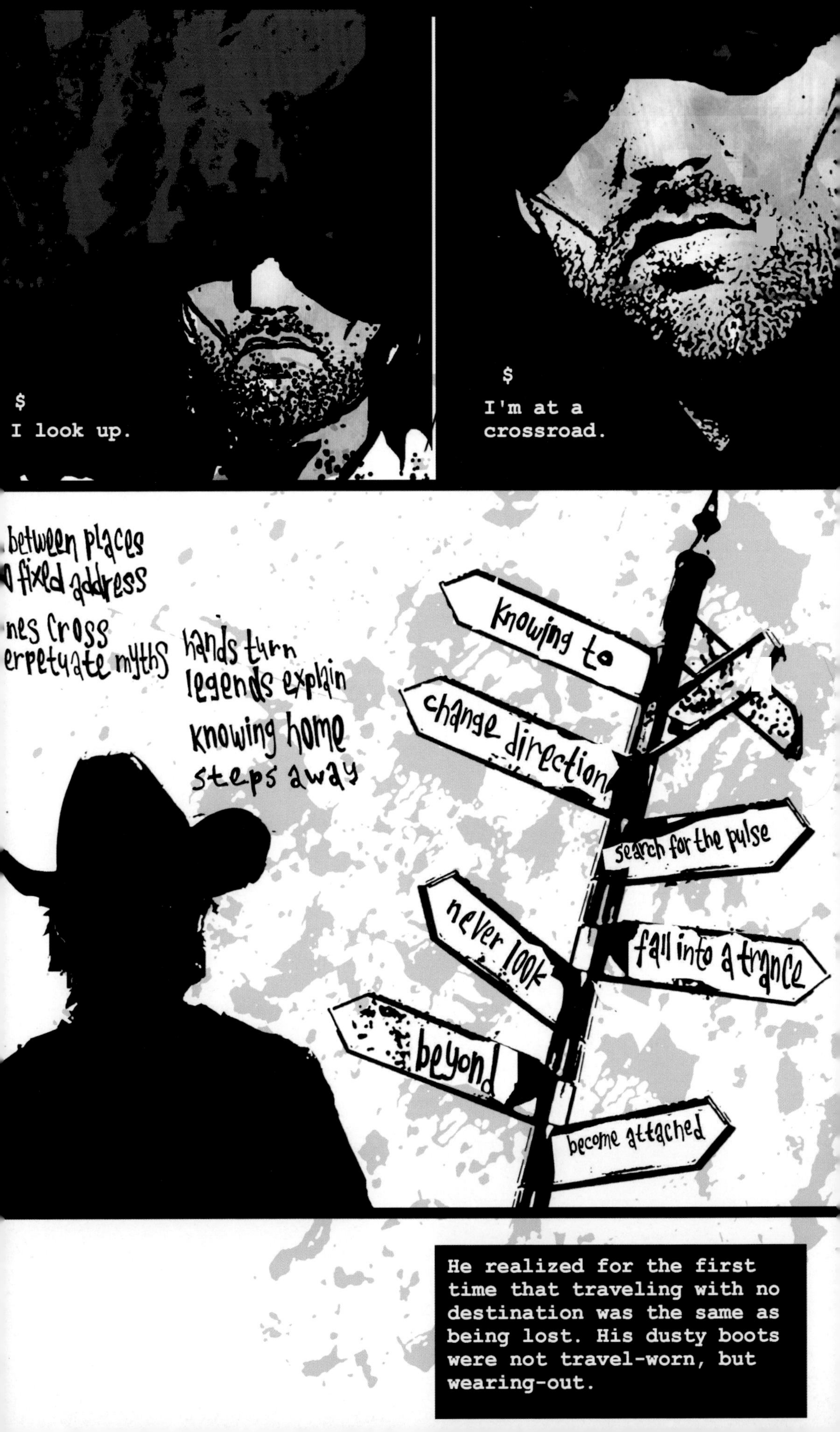
$
I look up.
$
I'm at a crossroad.
between places
o fixed address
nes cross
erpetuate myths
hands turn
legends explain
knowing home
steps away
knowing to
change direction
search for the pulse
never look
fall into a trance
beyond
become attached
He realized for the first time that traveling with no destination was the same as being lost. His dusty boots were not travel-worn, but wearing-out.

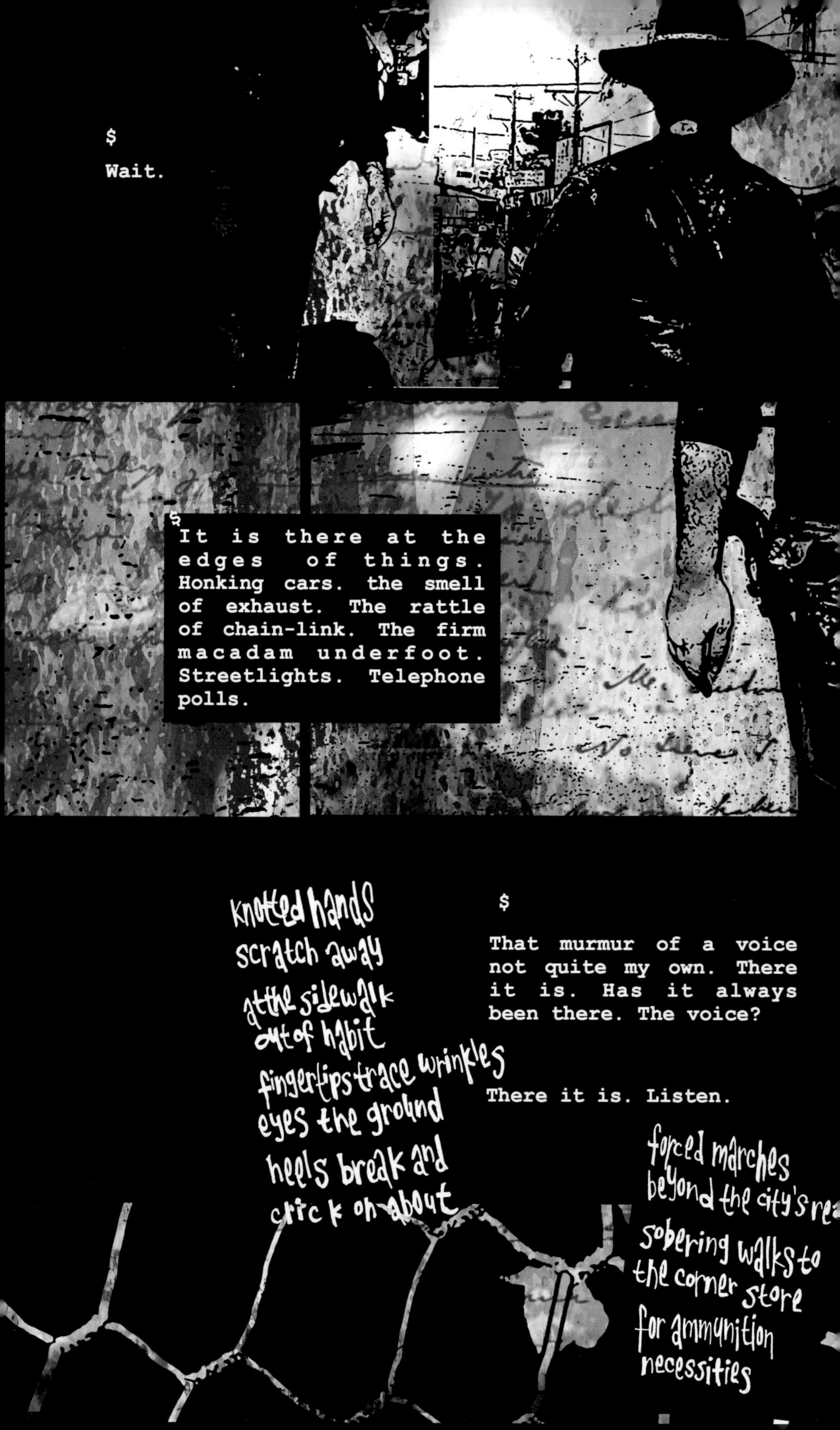
$
Wait.
$
It is there at the edges of things. Honking cars. the smell of exhaust. The rattle of chain-link. The firm macadam underfoot. Streetlights. Telephone polls.
knotted hands
scratch away
at the sidewalk
out of habit
fingertips trace wrinkles
eyes the ground
heels break and
crick on about
$
That murmur of a voice not quite my own. There it is. Has it always been there. The voice?
There it is. Listen.
forced marches
beyond the city's rea
sobering walks to
the corner store
for ammunition
necessities

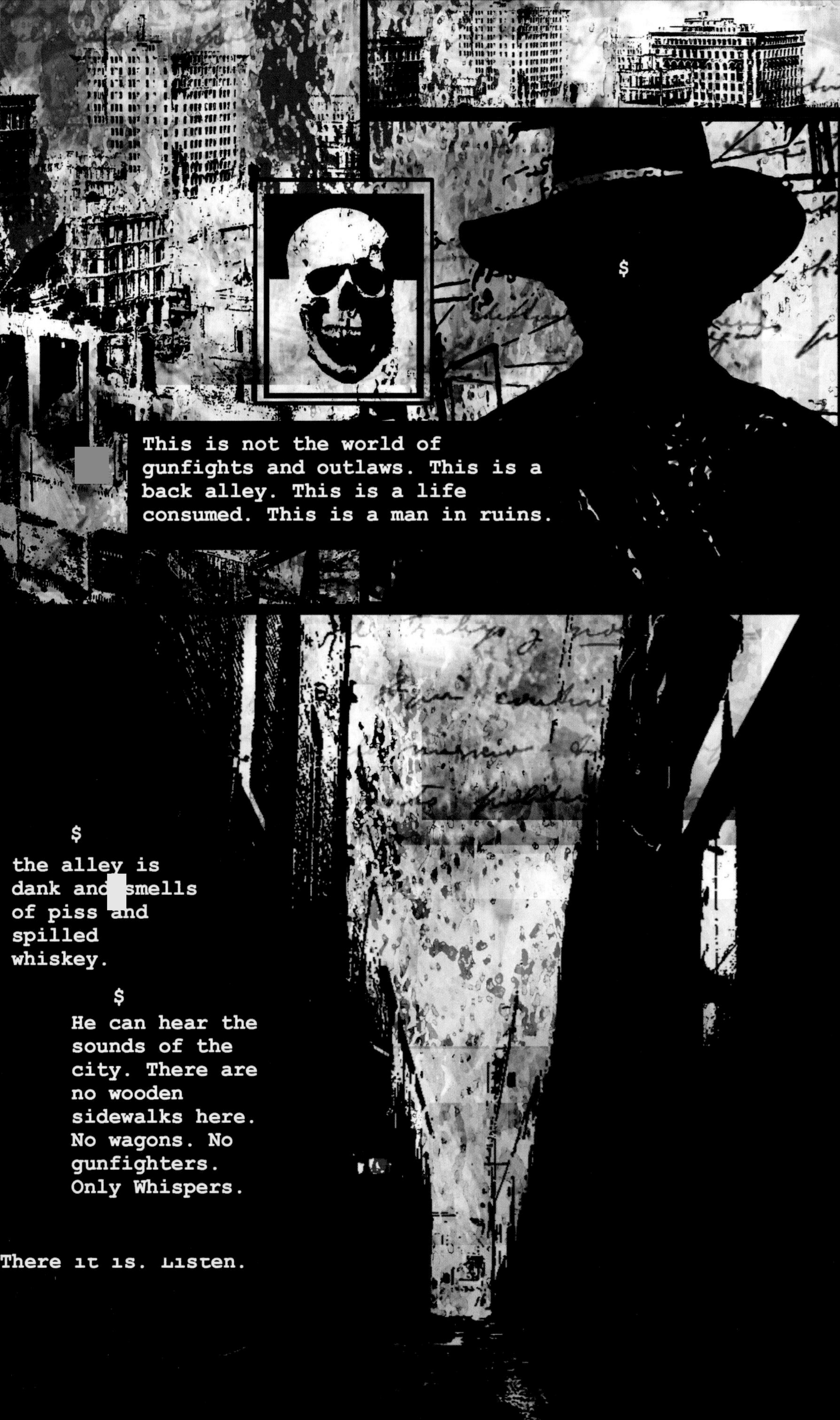
This is not the world of gunfights and outlaws. This is a back alley. This is a life consumed. This is a man in ruins.
the alley is dank and smells of piss and spilled whiskey.
He can hear the sounds of the city. There are no wooden sidewalks here. No wagons. No gunfighters. Only Whispers.
There it is. Listen.

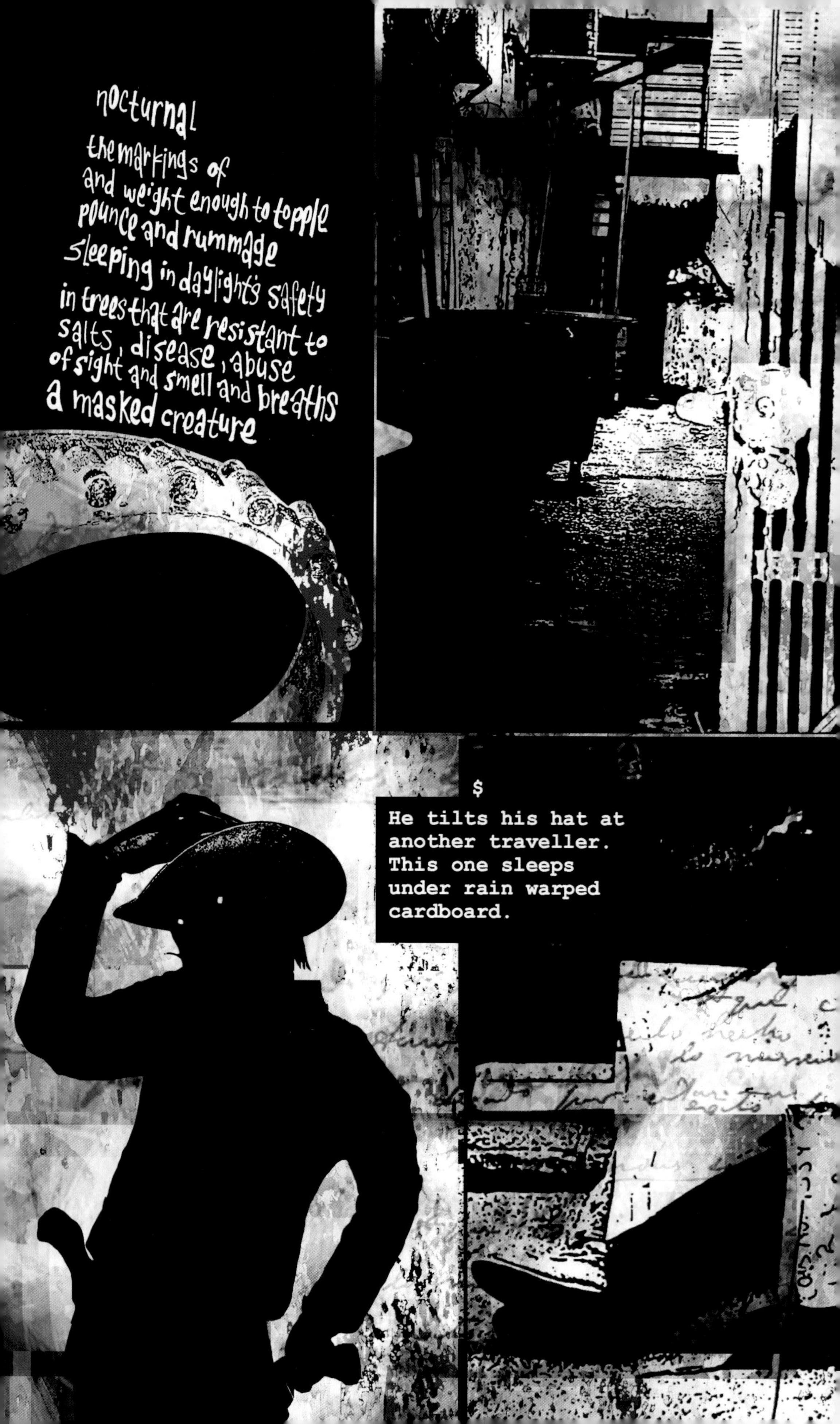
nocturnal
the markings of
and weight enough to topple
pounce and rummage
sleeping in daylight's safety
in trees that are resistant to
salts, disease, abuse
of sight and smell and breaths
a masked creature
$
He tilts his hat at another traveller. This one sleeps under rain warped cardboard.

$ *tail between the legs*

He hears the coo of
a soiled dove. She
tells him she's
been waiting.

a roll in the hay?

"There is too much
of the road on you
traveller" she
says.

used and useless, she spits
he spits back
high tails it out of there

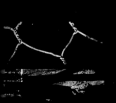

feet steady
all is quiet
on the horizon
no place but
away from here
peers over, leansin
things are looking up
like dandelions

$
The bus honks and he stumbles out of
the way. His clothing, filthy layers
he has found or taken. Be puts them
on over each other, imagines they
are riding leathers, chaps, a long
duster.

$
He drops the bottle, empty and the
glass chirps at him from the
pavement. It doesn't break. the
fighter doesn't fall.

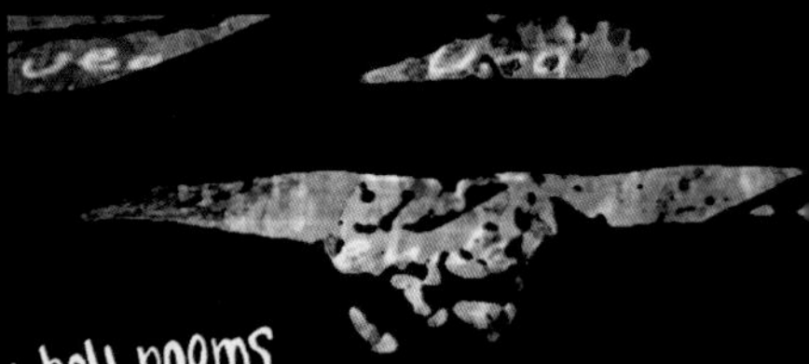

He adjusts his gun-belt, the irons
ready.

those cowboy poems
where will they emerge
in a higher voice and through another grin
he begins to speak with his hands
talk over the others and
lead 'em down the garden path

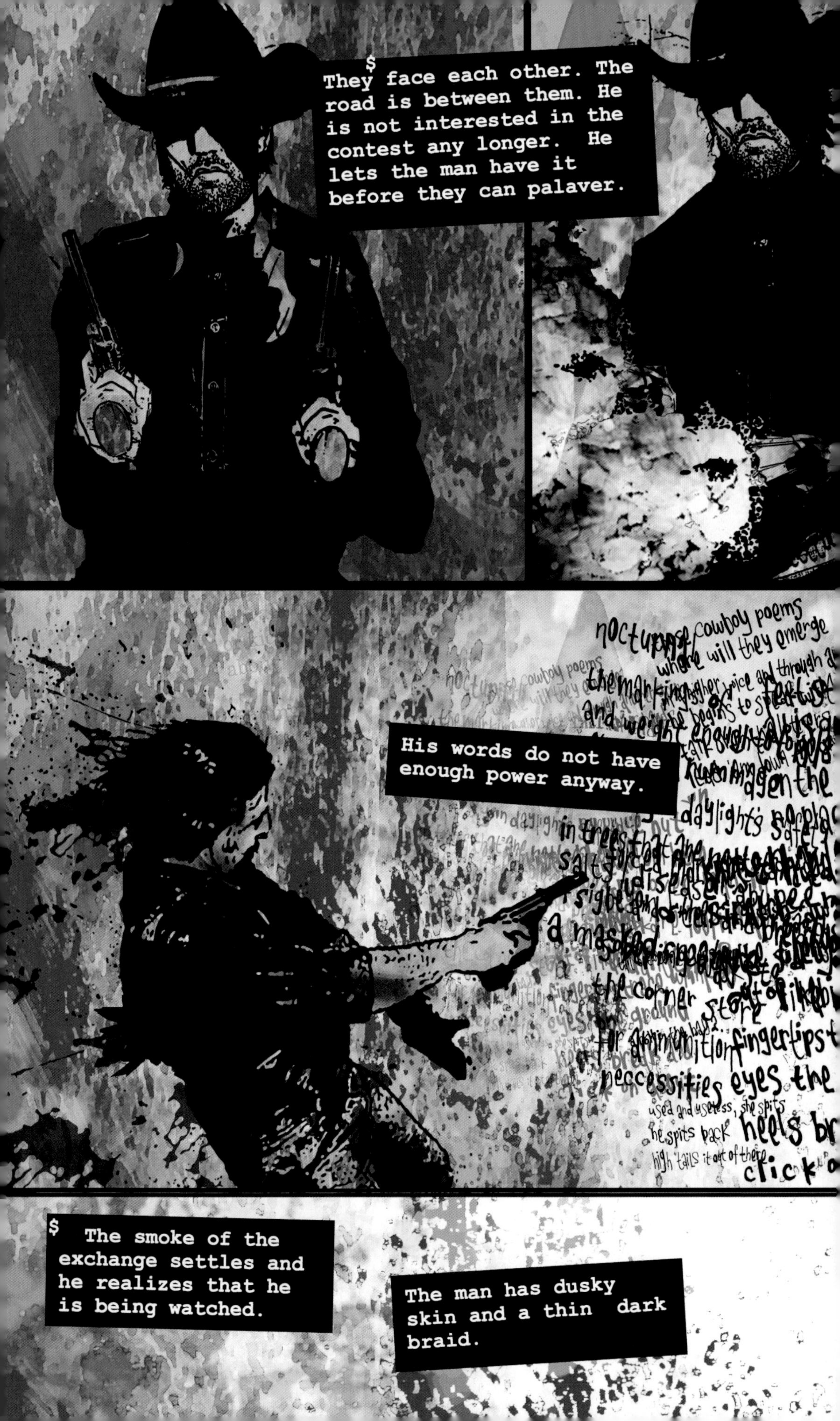
$ They face each other. The road is between them. He is not interested in the contest any longer. He lets the man have it before they can palaver.
His words do not have enough power anyway.
where will they emerge
daylights
the corner
for ammunition fingertips
neccessities eyes the
used and useless, she spits
he spits back
heels
high tails it out of there
click
$ The smoke of the exchange settles and he realizes that he is being watched.
The man has dusky skin and a thin dark braid.

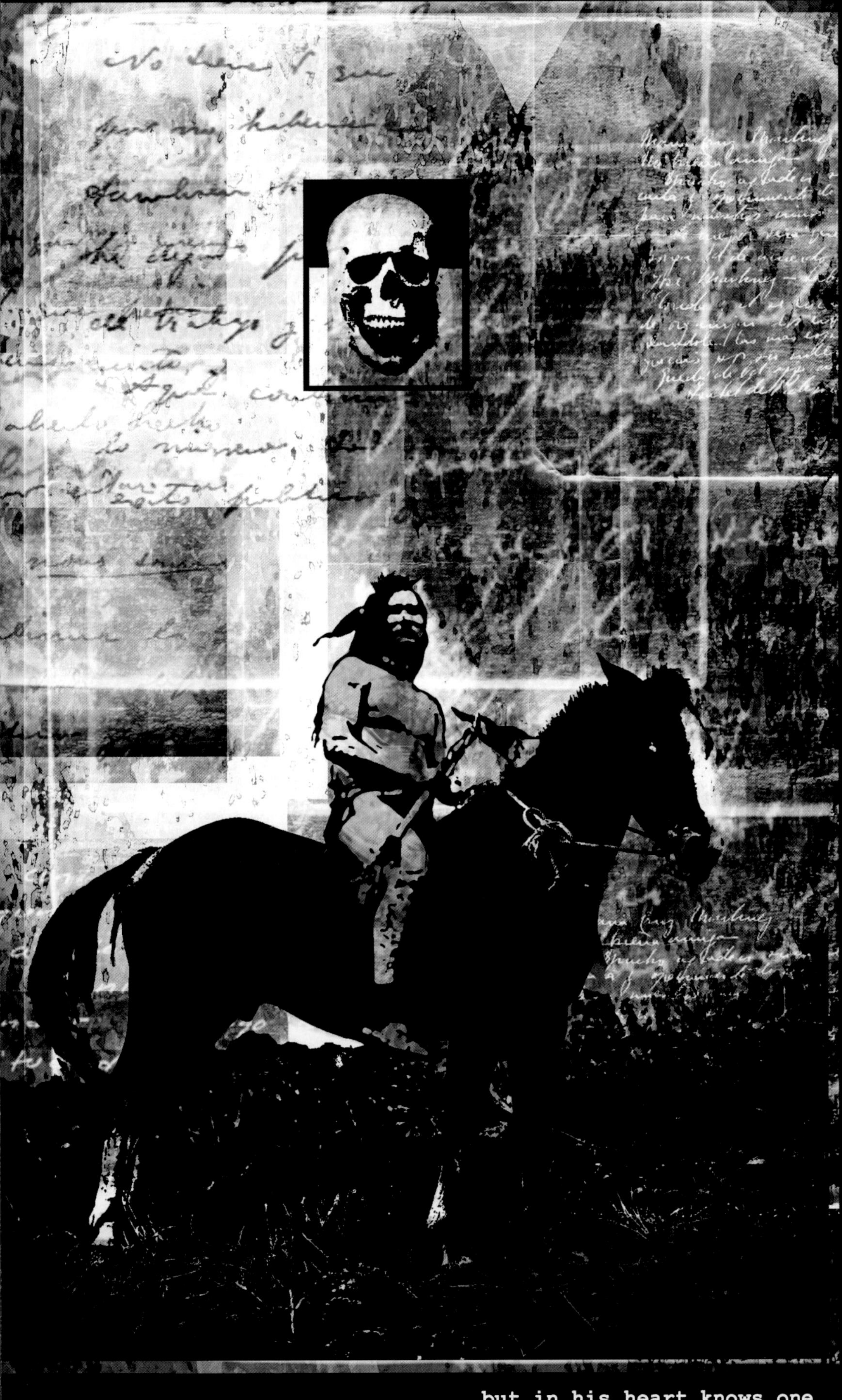

e dreams of cowboys and indians...

but in his heart knows one is gone forever.

not like that
not here anymore so
best explain how

you found yourself

in my winnipeg

from back where you came

no coincidence
midway between neither
here nor there nor

simple pursuits
the spin of a wheel
he thumbs the pages

answers a question
with a question, he poses
and this time they come running

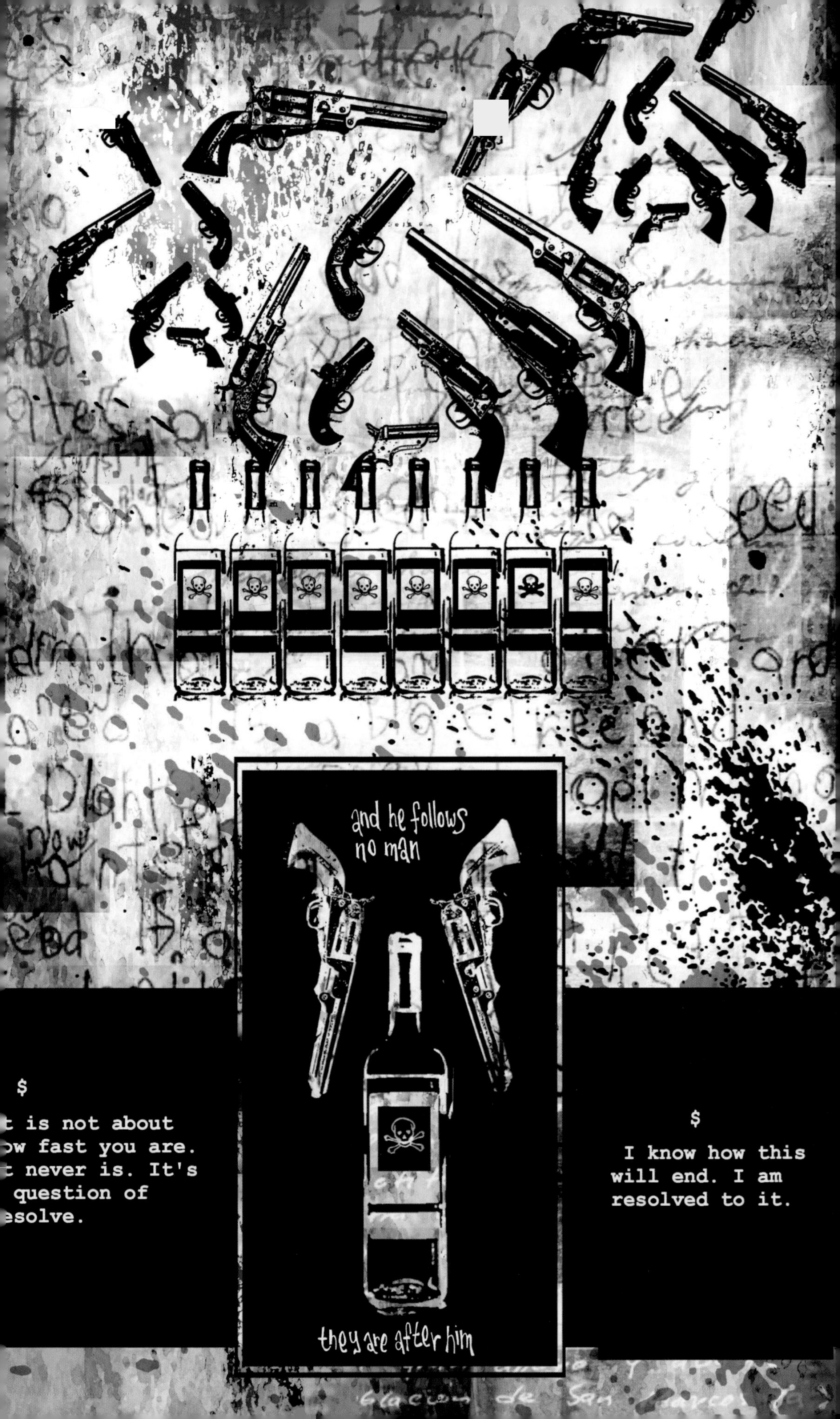
and he follows
no man
they are after him
$
t is not about
ow fast you are.
t never is. It's
question of
esolve.
$
I know how this
will end. I am
resolved to it.

He turns to face the dream. He must face it to escape. To survive.

intruding on the evening the iron horse to stand up to when souvenir spoons tinkle

In Langside he has his first real showdown. It isn't noon but that's what people will say. He doesn't think he knows the man, but people will say they were enemies from Star city. The bandit comes round on him from beside a wagon, shotgun up and ready. The bandit spooks the horse that's tethered there which spins, just as he lets loose both barrels. The horse takes the shots hard and full and falls backward. The man has his pistol up by then, which fires once, catching the bandit in the stomach. He backs away, then runs. It's a fair shooting people will say, but the horse's owner does not agree.

city growing bothered and forgetful of roaming blackouts he doubles back snorts braces himself

Somehow he is on the wrong side of law. These are marshals, he can tell from their blue uniforms and badges. There is a mistake. He is no outlaw. He has a white hat. He is a good guy. The marshals are going to take him.

The dream is that he is a dusty cowboy on a lonely trail.

He knows what they will do if they catch him.

He remembers the gamblers words:

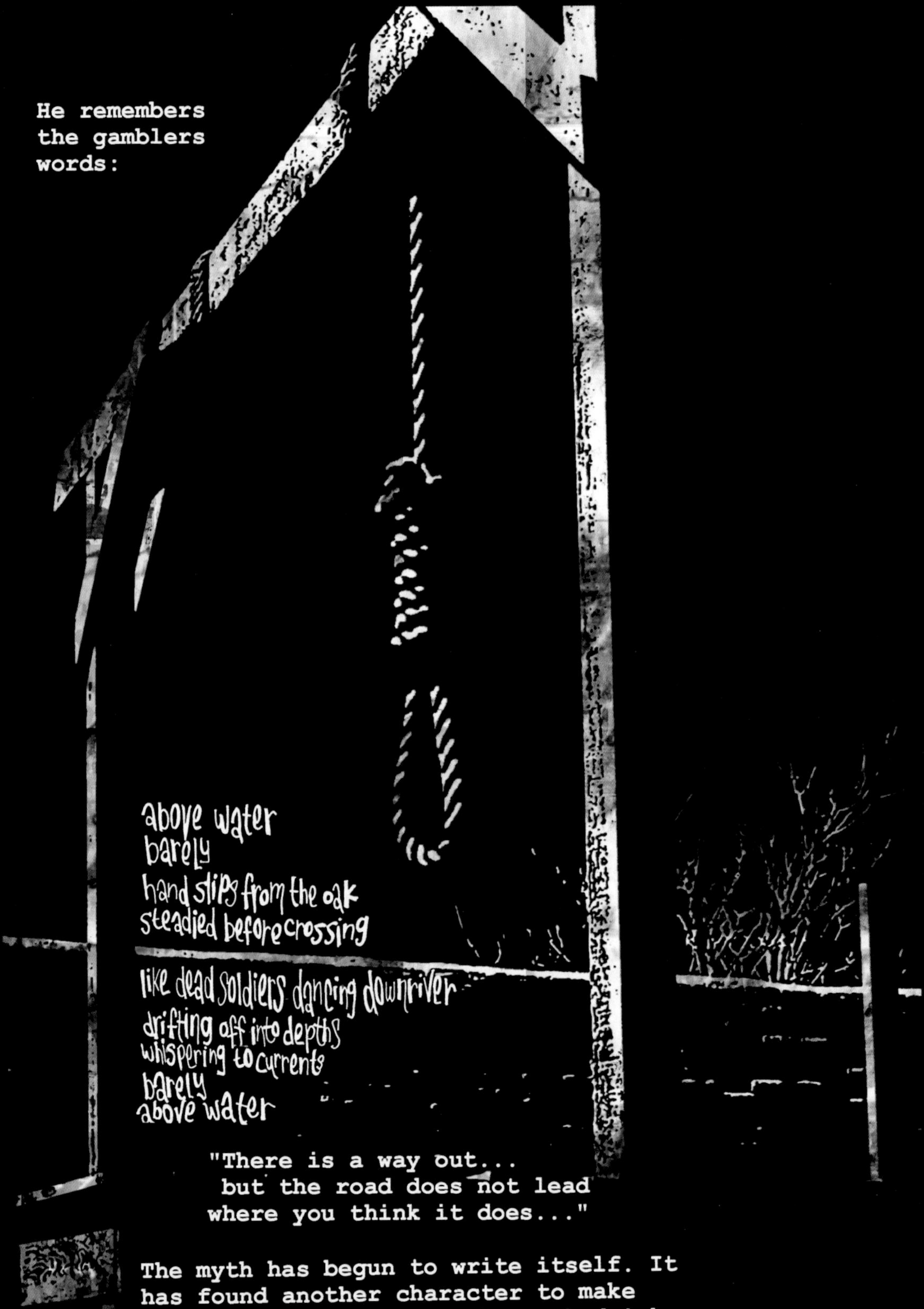
above water
barely
hand slips from the oak
steadied before crossing
like dead soldiers dancing downriver
drifting off into depths
whispering to currents
barely
above water

"There is a way out...
but the road does not lead
where you think it does..."

The myth has begun to write itself. It has found another character to make simple. Plain and dry. The myth drinks them both dry, and leaves a drought of reason.

Sirens call out into the night. police cruisers circle like pioneer wagons. "Police. Put your weapons down. Put your--"

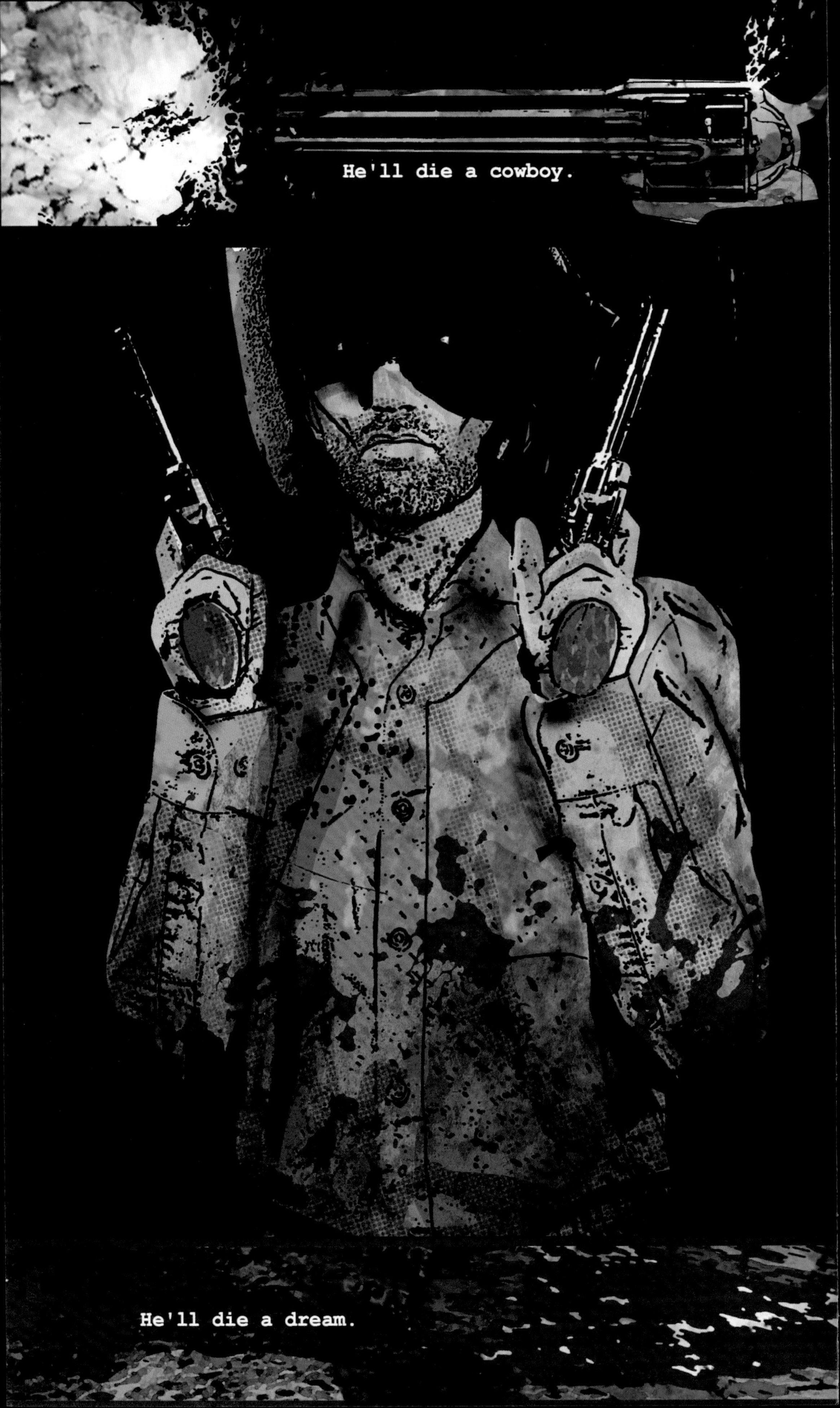
He'll die a cowboy.
He'll die a dream.

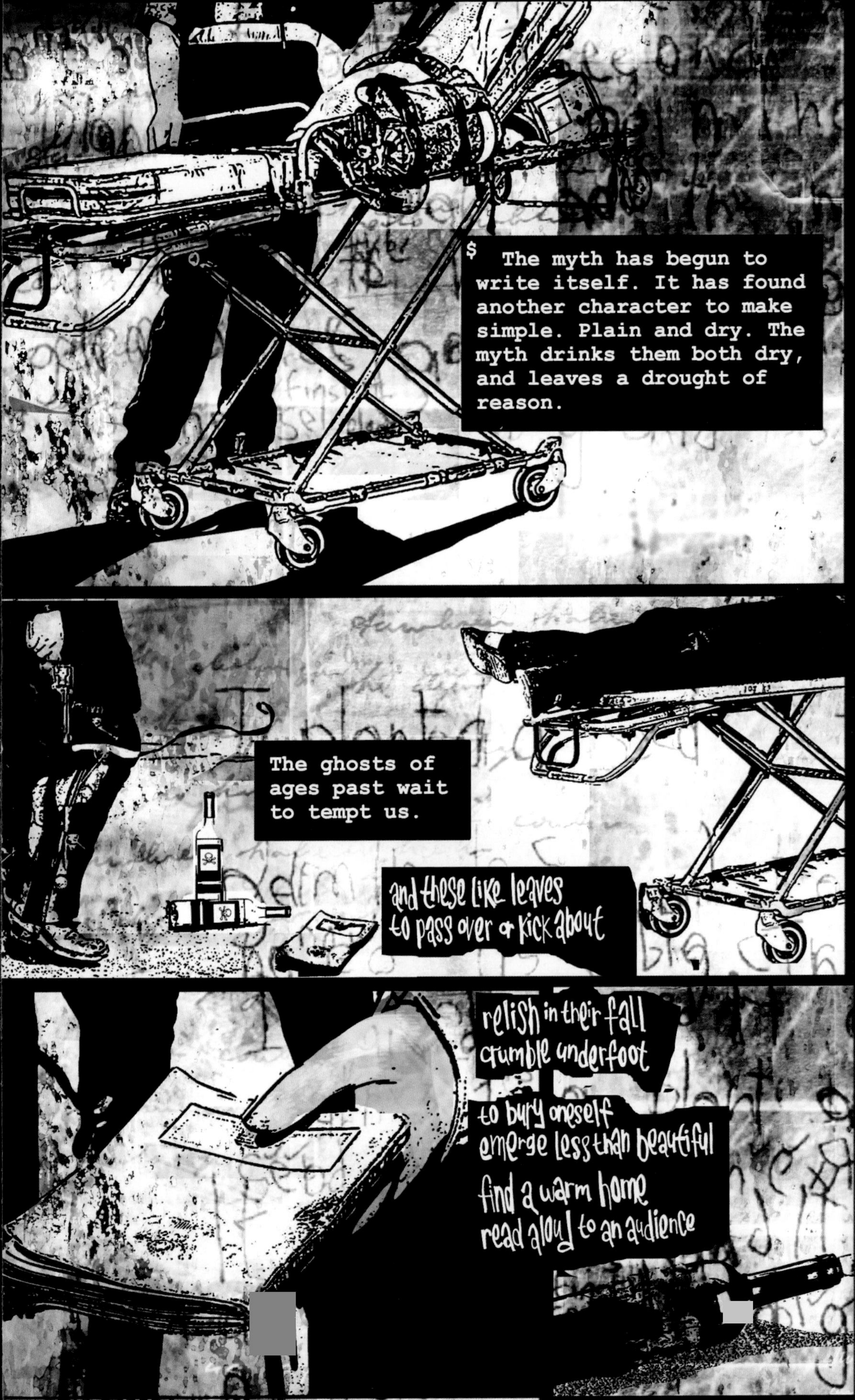
$ The myth has begun to write itself. It has found another character to make simple. Plain and dry. The myth drinks them both dry, and leaves a drought of reason.
The ghosts of ages past wait to tempt us.
and these like leaves
to pass over or kick about
relish in their fall
crumble underfoot
to bury oneself
emerge less than beautiful
find a warm home
read aloud to an audience

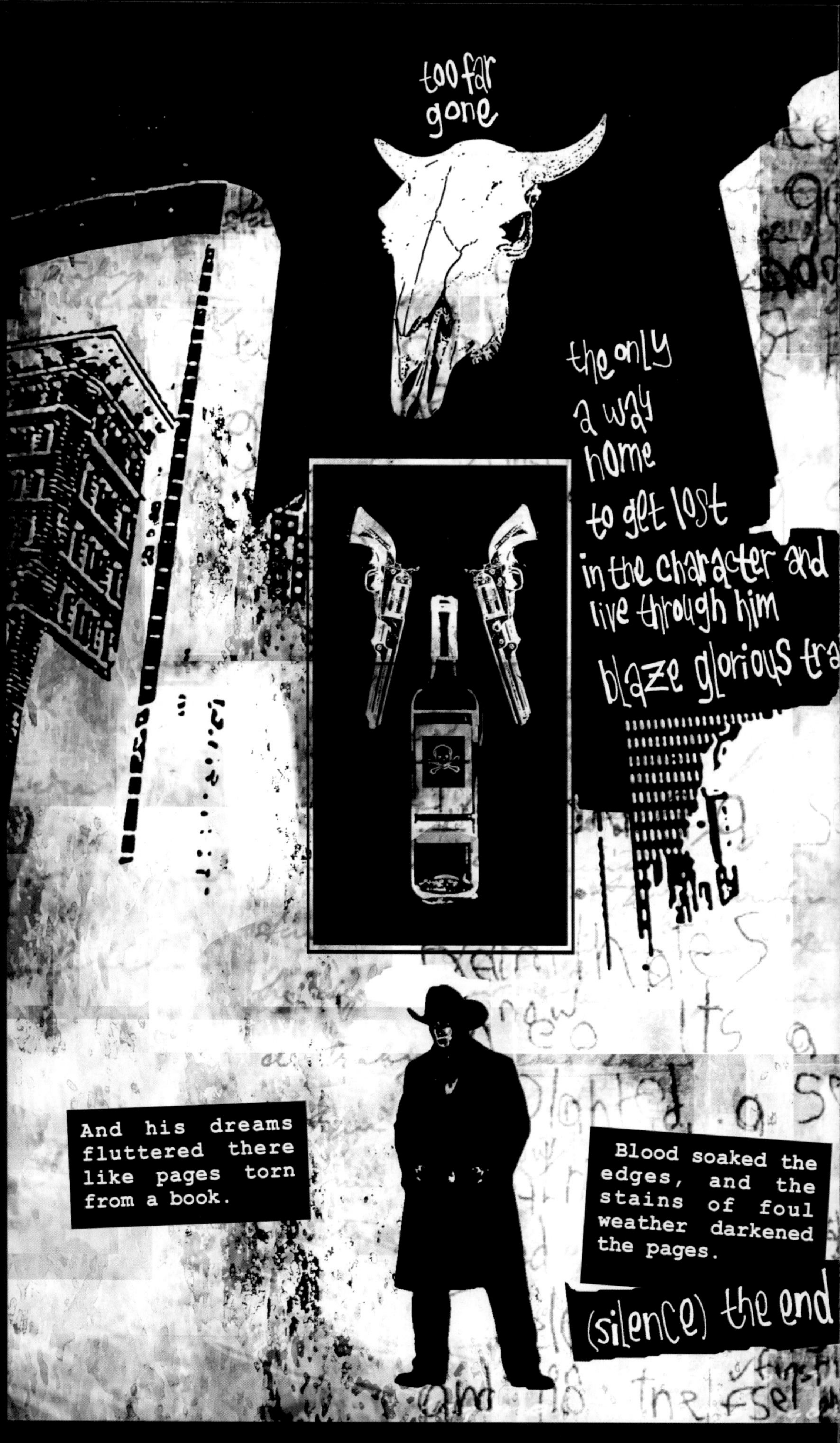
too far gone
the only
a way
home
to get lost
in the character and
live through him
blaze glorious tra
And his dreams fluttered there like pages torn from a book.
Blood soaked the edges, and the stains of foul weather darkened the pages.
(silence) the end

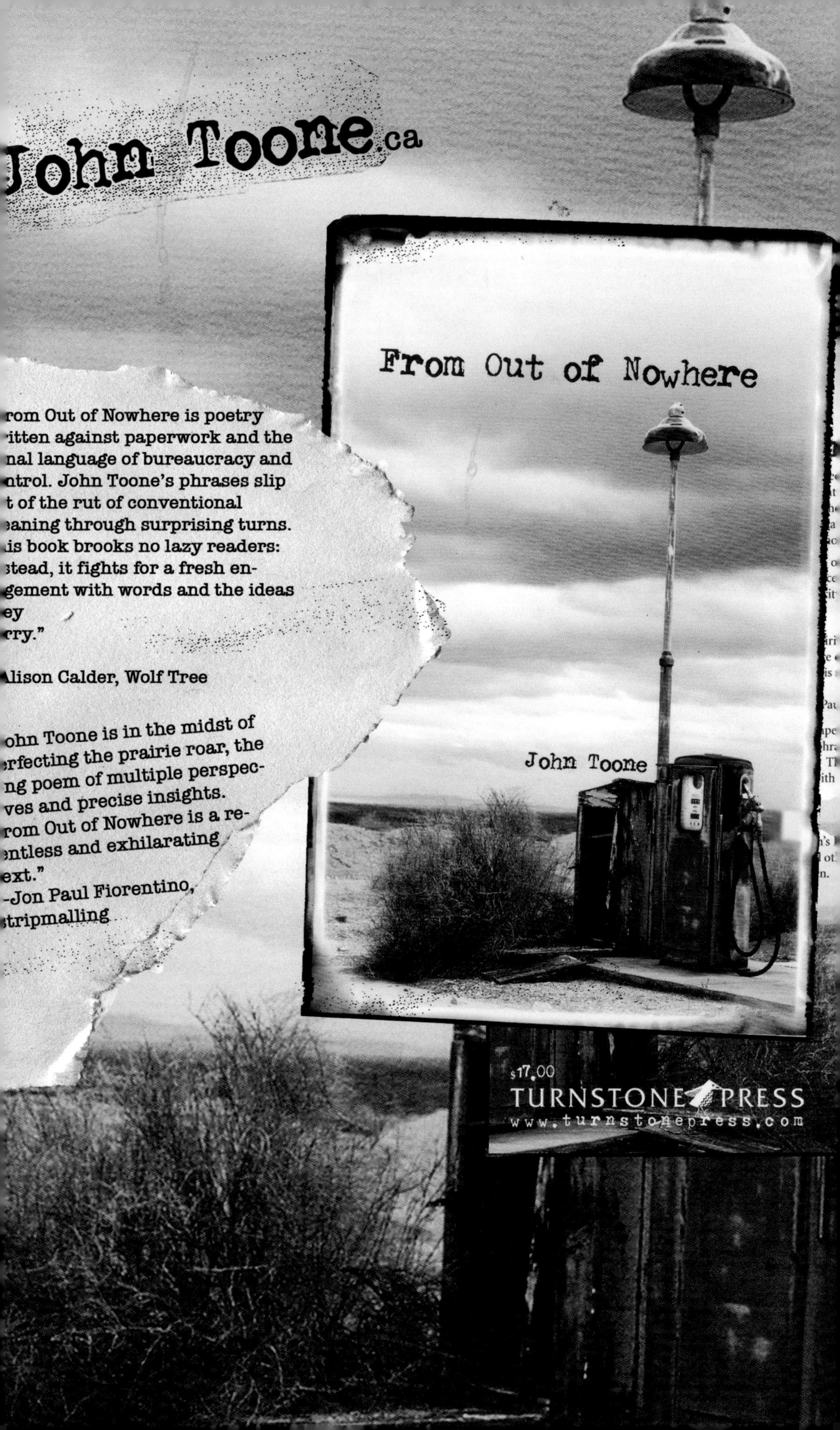
John Toone.ca
From Out of Nowhere
John Toone
rom Out of Nowhere is poetry
ritten against paperwork and the
nal language of bureaucracy and
ntrol. John Toone's phrases slip
t of the rut of conventional
eaning through surprising turns.
is book brooks no lazy readers:
stead, it fights for a fresh en-
gement with words and the ideas
ey
rry."
Alison Calder, Wolf Tree
ohn Toone is in the midst of
erfecting the prairie roar, the
ng poem of multiple perspec-
ves and precise insights.
rom Out of Nowhere is a re-
entless and exhilarating
ext."
–Jon Paul Fiorentino,
stripmalling
$17.00
TURNSTONE PRESS
www.turnstonepress.com

THE WOUND WILL RELIEVE THE PRESSURE

"IT'S LIKE A SLOW BLEED OUT OF MADNESS, AGAINST A CITY OF STARK IMAGES, WHERE EVERYTHING LOOKS HAUNTED AND STRICKEN, AND COMPLICIT. AS THE FILM DRIPS SLOWLY INTO THE CAUSTIC ENDING, THE IMAGES GROW MORE HORRIBLE, MORE FRIGHTENING, EVERY ONE OF THEM SUITABLE FOR FRAMING."
SUSIE MALONEY ~ AUTHOR OF "THE DWELLING"

ABSURD MACHINE FILMS PRESENTS

AEGRI SOMNIA

A SICK MAN'S DREAMS

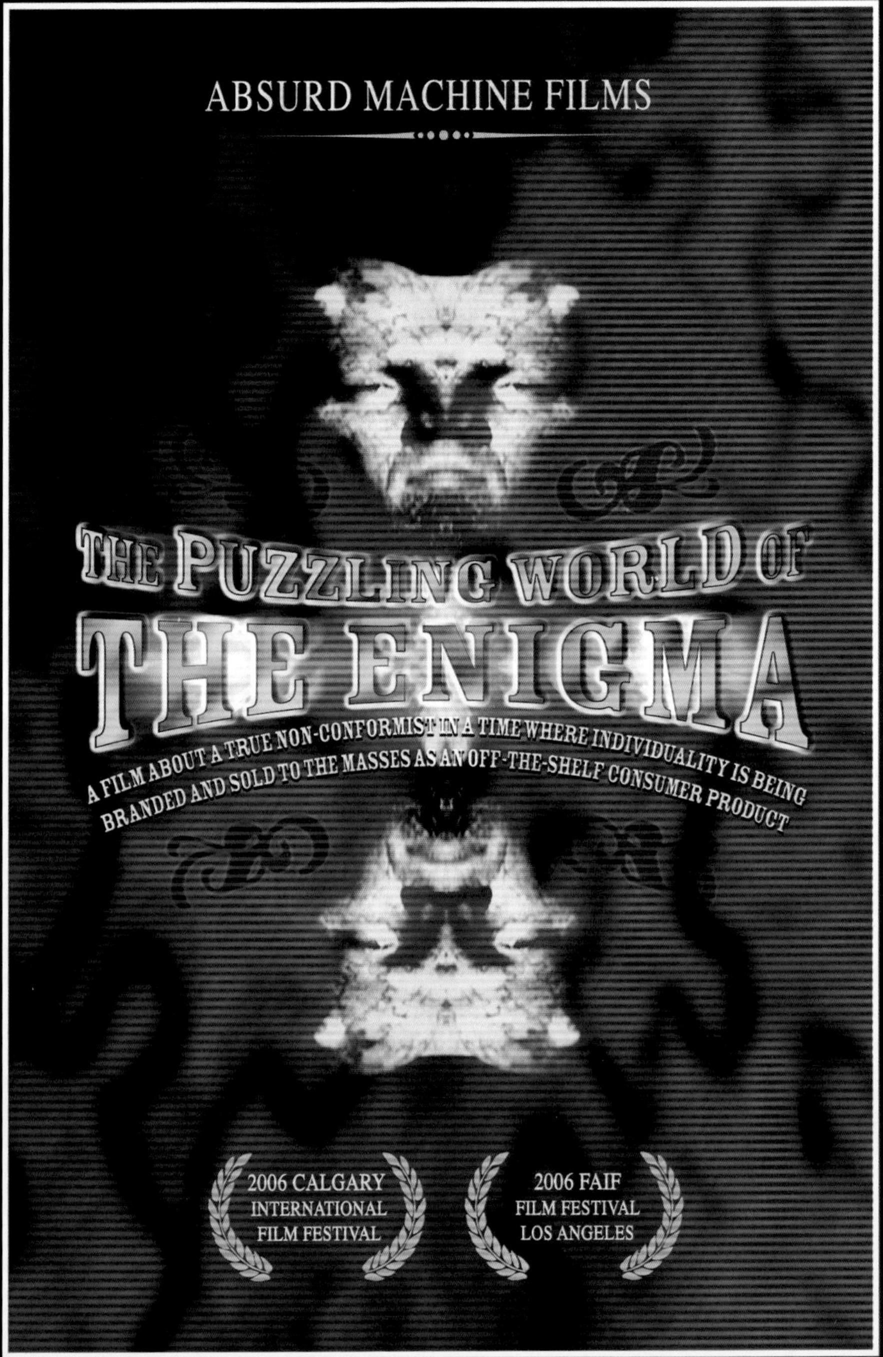
ABSURD MACHINE FILMS
THE PUZZLING WORLD OF
THE ENIGMA
A FILM ABOUT A TRUE NON-CONFORMIST IN A TIME WHERE INDIVIDUALITY IS BEING BRANDED AND SOLD TO THE MASSES AS AN OFF-THE-SHELF CONSUMER PRODUCT
2006 CALGARY INTERNATIONAL FILM FESTIVAL
2006 FAIF FILM FESTIVAL LOS ANGELES

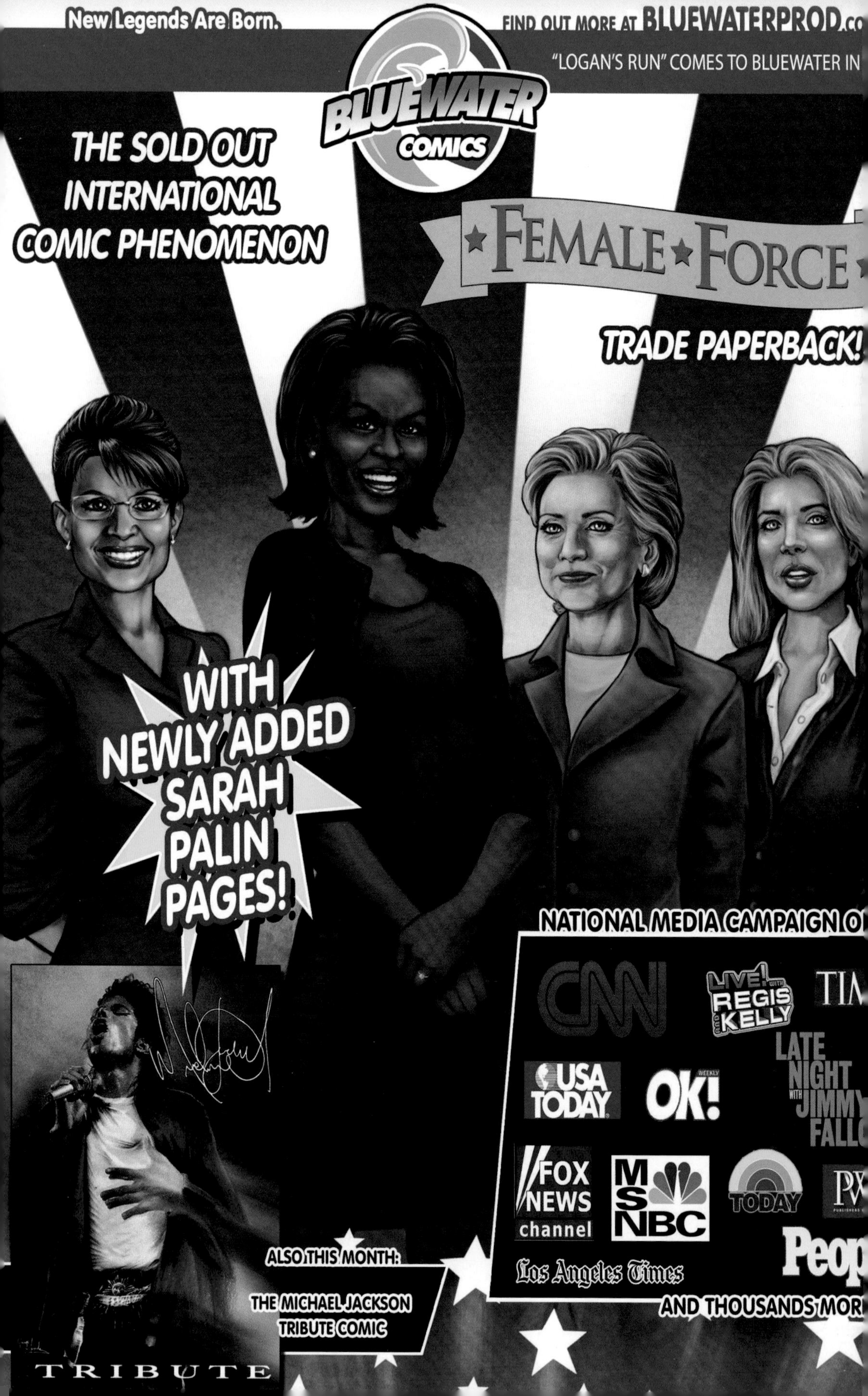

New Legends Are Born.
FIND OUT MORE AT BLUEWATERPROD.co
"LOGAN'S RUN" COMES TO BLUEWATER IN
BLUEWATER COMICS
THE SOLD OUT INTERNATIONAL COMIC PHENOMENON
FEMALE FORCE
TRADE PAPERBACK!
WITH NEWLY ADDED SARAH PALIN PAGES!
NATIONAL MEDIA CAMPAIGN O
CNN
LIVE! WITH REGIS AND KELLY
TIM
LATE NIGHT WITH JIMMY FALL
USA TODAY
OK! WEEKLY
FOX NEWS channel
MSNBC
TODAY
PW
Los Angeles Times
Peop
AND THOUSANDS MOR
ALSO THIS MONTH:
THE MICHAEL JACKSON TRIBUTE COMIC
TRIBUTE

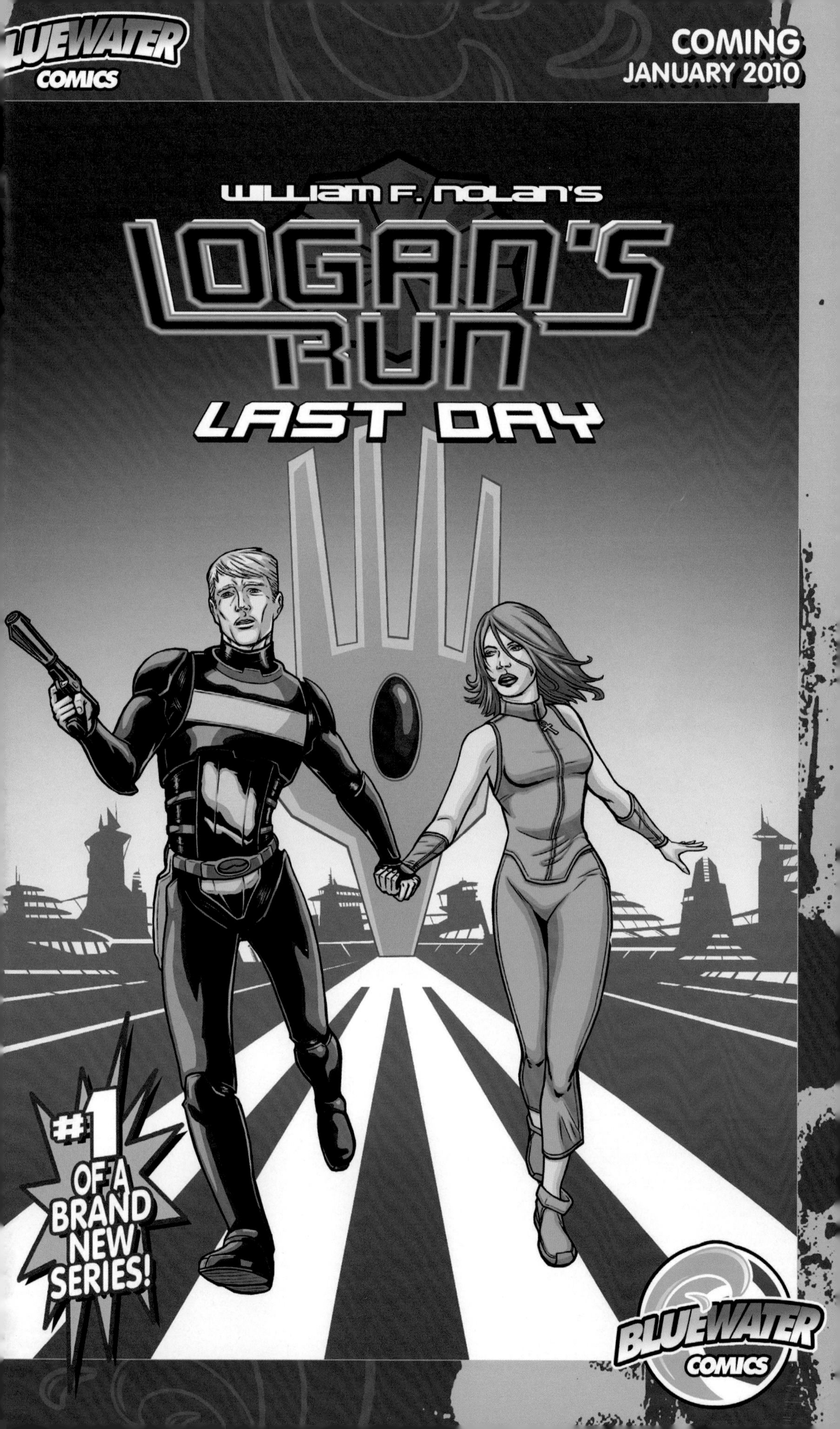
BLUEWATER COMICS
COMING JANUARY 2010
WILLIAM F. NOLAN'S
LOGAN'S RUN
LAST DAY
#1 OF A BRAND NEW SERIES!
BLUEWATER COMICS

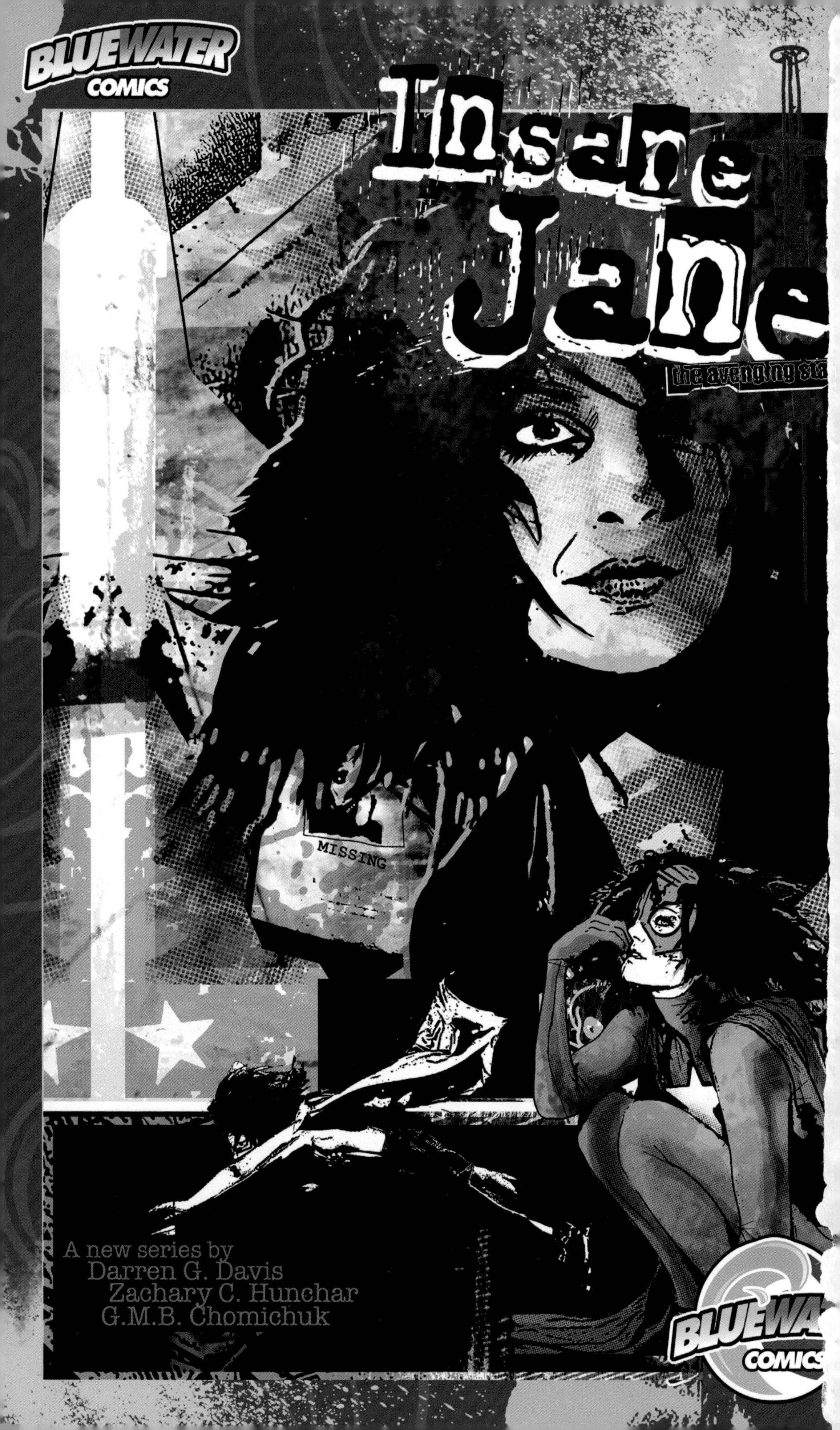
BLUEWATER COMICS
Insane Jane
the avenging sta
MISSING
A new series by
Darren G. Davis
Zachary C. Hunchar
G.M.B. Chomichuk
BLUEWATER COMICS

www.alchemicalpress.com

ALCHEMICAL
PRESS

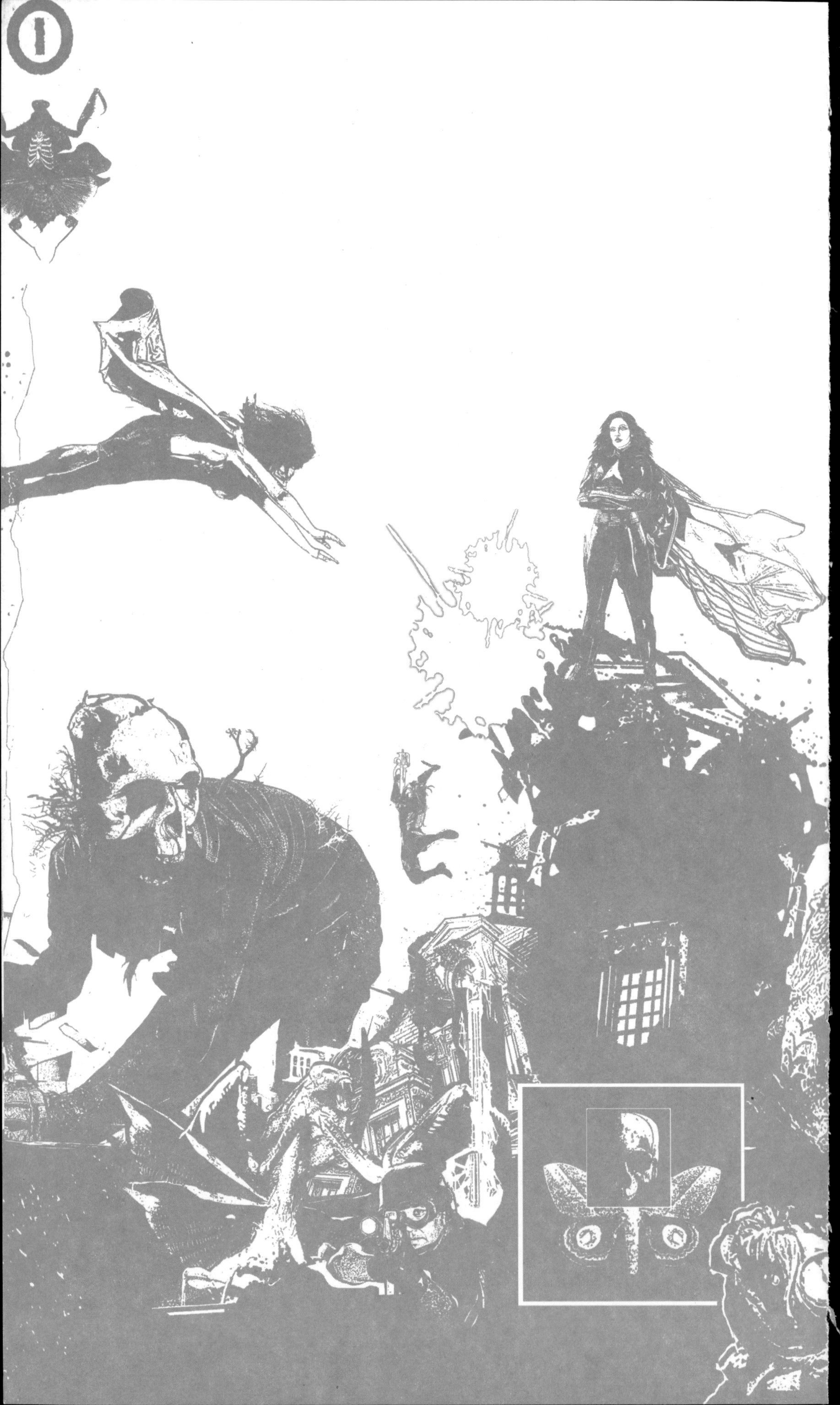